Women from Samburuland, Kenya, where the Samburu people struggle to maintain their traditional way of life

D1092709

YA
323
JOH

 # Contents

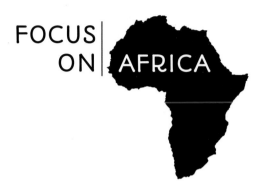

FOCUS ON AFRICA

Human Rights in Contemporary Africa

Anna Maria Johnson

Cavendish
Square

New York

RAP   3 2401 00903 512 4

Published in 2017 by Cavendish Square Publishing, LLC
243 5th Avenue, Suite 136, New York, NY 10016

Copyright © 2017 by Cavendish Square Publishing, LLC

First Edition

No part of this publication may be reproduced, stored in a retrieval system, or transmitted in any form or by any means—electronic, mechanical, photocopying, recording, or otherwise—without the prior permission of the copyright owner. Request for permission should be addressed to Permissions, Cavendish Square Publishing, 243 5th Avenue, Suite 136, New York, NY 10016. Tel (877) 980-4450; fax (877) 980-4454.

Website: cavendishsq.com

This publication represents the opinions and views of the author based on his or her personal experience, knowledge, and research. The information in this book serves as a general guide only. The author and publisher have used their best efforts in preparing this book and disclaim liability rising directly or indirectly from the use and application of this book.

CPSIA Compliance Information: Batch #CW17CSQ

All websites were available and accurate when this book was sent to press.

Library of Congress Cataloging-in-Publication Data

Names: Johnson, Anna Maria, author.
Title: Human rights in contemporary Africa / Anna Maria Johnson.
Other titles: Focus on Africa.
Description: New York : Cavendish Square Publishing, 2017. | Series: Focus on Africa | Includes bibliographical references and index.
Identifiers: LCCN 2016030597 (print) | LCCN 2016031128 (ebook) | ISBN 9781502623799 (library bound) | ISBN 9781502623805 (E-book)
Subjects: LCSH: Human rights--Africa. | Africa--Social conditions--21st century.
Classification: LCC JC599.A35 J64 2017 (print) | LCC JC599.A35 (ebook) | DDC 323.096--dc23
LC record available at https://lccn.loc.gov/2016030597

Editorial Director: David McNamara
Editor: Caitlyn Miller
Copy Editor: Michele Suchomel-Casey
Associate Art Director: Amy Greenan
Production Assistant: Karol Szymczuk
Photo Research: J8 Media

The photographs in this book are used by permission and through the courtesy of: Cover John Ferguson/Oxfam/CC BY 2.0; p. 4 Africanway/iStockphoto.com; p. 10 Robertharding/Alamy Stock Photo; p. 12 Wikimedia Commons/Jørn Sund-Henriksen/File:ElAiounrefugeecamp.jpg/CC BY 3.0; p. 16 GEOATLAS GRAPHIOGRE/Shutterstock.com; p. 17 Wikimedia Commons/File: Western sahara map showing morocco and polisaro/CC BY 3.0; p. 22 Fethi Belaid/AFP/Getty Images; p. 25 (top) Wolfgang Kaehler/LightRocket via Getty Images, (bottom) ABDULLAH DOMA/AFP/Getty Images; p. 29 UTOMI EKPEI/AFP/Getty Images; p. 34 Pichugin Dmitry/Shutterstock.com; p. 41 PHILIP OJISUA/AFP/Getty Images; p. 42 AFP/Getty Images; p. 45 Trevor Kittelty/Shutterstock.com; p. 46 Wikimedia Commons/USAID Africa Bureau/File:Education programs bring primary education to vulnerable and conflict-affected children in Uganda (7269658160).jpg/Public Domain; p. 53 Brian Sokol/Panos; p. 63WILLIAM DAVIES/AFP/Getty Images; p. 72 Ruby/Alamy Stock Photo; p. 76 Wikimedia Commons/AMISOM Public Information/File:2013 08 Belet Weyne Situation 015 (9625501747).jpg/Public Domain; p. 81 WALTER DHLADHLA/AFP/Getty Images; p. 87 Wikimedia Commons/K. Kendall/File:National Women's Day.jpg/CC BY 2.0; p. 89 Jason Edwards/National Geographic/Getty Images; p. 94 Courtesy UN Women/Ryan Brown; p. 96 Wikimedia Commons/Sara Atkins/File:Swaziland landscape.jpg/CC BY 2.0; p. 98 Danita Delimont/Alamy Stock Photo; p. 105 Wikimedia Commons/IICD (http://www.flickr.com/people/32348003@N02) from The Hague, The Netherlands/File:CFSU Nov2010 KyeizoobaGirls Bushenyi (41)/ (5348561907).jpg/CC BY 2.0; p. 109 DeAgostini/Getty Images; p. 110 File:Regions of the African Union.png/Wikipedia Commons.

Printed in the United States of America

Introduction

Basic and Universal Human Rights in Africa

It's difficult to escape discussions of **human rights**, and sometimes it can seem like human rights violations occur exclusively on particular continents. Often when we switch on the news and hear of war crimes or suppressed freedom of speech, an African nation is the focus of the story. In reality, human rights violations occur in every country—though many African countries struggle with human rights issues as political changes continue to sweep across the continent.

Before we take a look at the way human rights affect Africans, the relationships between African nations, and African countries' relationships with the world, we must first examine the global development of the concept of human rights.

All human beings are born with certain inalienable rights—rights that can never be taken away, though they can be violated—no matter their country of origin. This is not a new idea; people have had various notions of rights for a long time. The Magna Carta, national constitutions, and the Bill of Rights are examples of some of the attempts people have made to proclaim human rights.

So what are human rights exactly? The concept was carefully described and discussed after World War II, in the Declaration of Universal Human Rights. On December 10, 1948, in Paris, the United Nations General Assembly signed the document, which consists of thirty articles that list specific rights for all people. The first five articles provide a clear understanding of what activists and other stakeholders mean by the term "human rights":

Article 1.

All human beings are born free and equal in dignity and rights. They are endowed with reason and conscience and should act towards one another in a spirit of brotherhood.

Article 2.

Everyone is entitled to all the rights and freedoms set forth in this Declaration, without distinction of any kind, such as race, colour, sex, language, religion, political or other opinion, national or social origin, property, birth or other status. Furthermore, no distinction shall be made on the basis of the political, jurisdictional or international status of the country or territory to which a person belongs, whether it be independent, trust, non-self-governing or under any other limitation of sovereignty.

Article 3.

Everyone has the right to life, liberty and
security of person.

Article 4.

No one shall be held in slavery or servitude;
slavery and the slave trade shall be
prohibited in all their forms.

Article 5.

No one shall be subjected to **torture** or
to cruel, inhuman or degrading treatment
or punishment.

The Universal Declaration of Human Rights sets a very
high standard for how human beings should treat one another
and how they should expect to be treated. Crafted and signed
by leaders from many cultures, countries, and backgrounds,
it standardizes the rights, freedoms, and duties for all human
beings that deserve to be protected. An inspiring document,
it depicts a world where every person is worthy of having
equality, freedom, security, a basic standard of living, free
basic education, protection in old age and in sickness,
freedom to marry whom they choose, freedom to change
their religion or beliefs, and a responsibility to the community
to which they belong.

Although this declaration was called "universal," it was
not necessarily written with Africans in mind. Rather, those
who drafted the document in 1948 were responding to the
horrific events of world wars. They wished to set standards to
protect people from the kinds of abuses suffered under Nazi

Germany and Stalinist Russia, among others. At the same time, most of Africa did not yet have independent nations; various regions were governed piecemeal by other nations (empires) under **colonialism**, while within the African colonies, various and numerous tribes and kingdoms tried to function as they had in ancient times. It would take decades for the African colonies to become independent nations, and for the world to perceive Africans as having the same inalienable rights described in the declaration.

During the process of **decolonization**, in the 1950s to 1970s, the Organization for African Unity (OAU) formed to work toward the powerful human rights goal of gaining independence for each African country so that they would have the right of self-determination and to choose their own government.

After colonization, the OAU evolved into what is today called the African Union (AU), a body that unites all the countries of Africa (except Morocco, which has a unique status that will be discussed in chapter 1). The AU wrote a document to proclaim human rights for African people, called the African Charter on Human and Peoples' Rights. Although similar to the Universal Declaration of Human Rights, it states duties and responsibilities in addition to rights.

Imperialism (the attempt by sovereign nations to expand their reach into other lands) and colonialism have contributed to both problems and solutions to human rights issues in Africa. The transition from colony status to independence was smoother for some nations than for others. For some nations, the transition is not yet complete, as fledgling nations require time to become established.

This book looks at human rights today in the face of these transitions. We will examine each of the five regions of the continent, according to the African Union's definition of northern, western, central, eastern, and southern Africa. Today fifty-four countries (at most recent count) comprise Africa; these diverse nations each face unique obstacles as they grapple with issues of human safety, security, and dignity. However, within Africa, local people offer perspectives and solutions that humanitarian aid groups and relief organizations might not have considered. Often the best and most effective solutions will come from local Africans because they best understand their culture, communities, value, and history.

The Tuareg are an indigenous, seminomadic people who live and travel in parts of Algeria, Mali, Niger, Burkina Faso, and Nigeria.

1 | Northern Africa

Northern Africa, located next to the Middle East, has been a particularly fascinating region during the past several years. Multiple revolutions, transitional governments, brand-new constitutions, and human rights progress (as well as a few steps back) have made northern Africa a region to watch.

Though Africa calls to mind sub-Saharan African jungles and savannas, the northern part of the continent includes the Maghreb, which borders the Mediterranean Sea; the Sahara Desert; and the eastern part of the Sahel, a semiarid zone. Northern Africa is rich in oil, in ancient history, in stunning coastal cities, and in people groups, including the **Berbers** (the region's earliest inhabitants), **Arabs** (who joined the region around the seventh century), and black Africans (from farther south) who presently make their homes in Egypt, Libya, Tunisia, Morocco, Algeria, Mauritania, and the Saharawi Arab Democratic Republic (SADR). The many different languages, religions, traditions, and cultural practices represented in the region provide richness and beauty—as well as opportunities for conflict.

The countries bordering the Mediterranean Sea include the SADR, Morocco, Algeria, Tunisia, and Libya and are collectively known as the Maghreb. Mauritania is located

Tindouf refugee camp in Algeria, where many of the Saharawi people have lived for forty years

nearby but is described as part of the Sahel, a swath of land that forms a transitional zone between the Sahara Desert to the north and the humid savannas to the south. Some coastal areas of Algeria and Tunisia are also considered to be part of the Sahel. (The other countries of the Sahel will be discussed in subsequent chapters because they are part of western, central, and eastern Africa; the Sahel stretches across the width of the continent, including parts of Senegal, Mali, Burkina Faso, Niger, Nigeria, Chad, and the Sudan).

Northern Africa is often grouped with the Middle Eastern countries because of its close proximity and its heavy Arab influence. For example, the websites of organizations like the United Nations and Human Rights Watch include "North Africa & Middle East" together on their site maps but place the remainder of Africa in a separate category, called sub-Saharan Africa. The Sahara Desert has served as a kind of barrier, separating the cultures of northern Africa from the more southern countries. Because the Mediterranean Sea has connected northern Africa to the Middle East, these regions in some ways have more in common with one another than with sub-Saharan Africa.

Northern Africa is a treasure trove of incredibly rich heritage, including the pyramids of Egypt, ornate mosques in Algeria, historical figures such as the Queen of Sheba and Queen Nefertiti, belly dancing, Mediterranean food, and the earliest alphabets. This is where human history, as we know it, began.

Recently, a series of revolutions called the Arab Spring swept across the Maghreb and the Sahel. Beginning with a street vendor in Tunisia who set himself on fire in December 2010, the "Jasmine Revolution" swept Tunisian president Zine el-Abidine Ben Ali out of power. By January 25, 2011, revolution had also reached Egypt, forcing that nation's president, Hosni Mubarak, out of office and precipitating a new constitution for that country. During the same time, Algerians began protesting over food shortages, which pushed the government to end a nineteen-year-old state of emergency that had severely restricted personal freedoms. By February of that same year, Moroccan activists' protests led to a new constitution as well—and a demand for greater promotion of human rights. Meanwhile, in Libya, revolution overthrew Muammar Gaddafi after more than forty years of dictatorship. Unfortunately, the toppling of the authoritarian government that held power for more than four decades left a power vacuum. This has allowed regional terrorist groups and transnational criminals free reign to terrorize Libyan people. It may be many years before Libyan society regains stability and rule of law.

After so much change, the governments of northern Africa are fragile and struggle to maintain security, which is a necessary foundation for the protection of human rights. All of this revolutionary tumult has turned the attention of global citizens to the human rights situations in northern Africa. Civil unrest and human rights are closely related; where human rights are violated, protests can follow. Conversely, when people protest, their rights are more at risk of being violated, too. In order to bring stability to society, both sides of the coin—*security* and *human rights*—must be addressed.

The SADR

The African Union includes every African country with one exception: Morocco. Morocco was originally part of the African Union until it seceded over the controversy about Western Sahara, a territory Morocco occupies but which considers itself to be an independent (sovereign) nation called the Saharawi Arab Democratic Republic (SADR). To make matters more complicated, the United Nations (UN) refers to the Saharawi Arab Democratic Republic as a "non-self-governing territory." Some sources refer to the SADR as the last colony of Africa—in part because it was the last African colony to be set free from European imperialism, and in part because it still is not fully recognized as sovereign. More than eighty of the world's nations recognize the SADR as a country, but many do not (the United States, for example, does not).

Currently, the Saharwi Arab Democratic Republic is identified on Western-style maps as "Western Sahara, administered by Morocco." Previously, this region was known as Spanish Sahara when it was a Spanish protectorate (1884–1975).

The Origins of Morocco's Hold on the Western Sahara/SADR

Since many of today's human rights issues correspond to prior colonialism, it is necessary to consider the effect of events in the late 1800s and early 1900s on Africa today. By the start of the twentieth century, nearly all of the continent of Africa was claimed by various European nations bent on extracting its rich natural resources and exerting Western influence over African peoples.

In fact, in 1914, only Ethiopia and Liberia were self-governing (and Liberia had been created by an American society aiming to resettle former American slaves back in Africa, so it wasn't without external influence). Northern Africa was claimed, in various pieces, by France, Italy, and Britain. What are now Algeria, Mauritania, Tunisia, and Morocco were colonies of France, while Italy held Libya, and Britain claimed Egypt. Spain held part of Sahara (today's SADR/Western Sahara) until 1975, making it the last colony in Africa. When Spain finally agreed to relinquish its protectorate, however, it crafted an illegal agreement with Morocco and Mauritania: Spain agreed to join with Morocco and Mauritania with the understanding that the three nations would together control Western Sahara's future. Then Spain stepped out, leaving the other two countries in charge. The Saharawi people, on the other hand, desired self-governance and began to fight for independence. This led to a sixteen-year war. Mauritania relinquished its hold relatively quickly, but Morocco occupies the territory to this day.

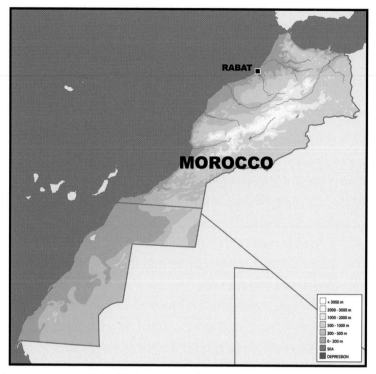

Moroccan maps include all of Western Sahara.

It is interesting to compare maps made by different seats of power. The website for the government of Morocco depicts the whole of Morocco plus the SADR/Western Sahara as simply "Morocco," bordered by Algiers (Algeria) and Mauritania.

Because of the unclear status of the SADR, most of the Saharawi people have been living for forty years in refugee camps in the neighboring countries of Algeria and Mauritania, and in the thin strip of the non-occupied portion of Western Sahara. Morocco has built a sand and stone wall, or berm, that stretches the entire length of the SADR from its border with Morocco to its southern border with Mauritania, dividing the country so that the western two-thirds (on the coastal side) is separated from the inland one-third (which is virtually unoccupied desert where agriculture is impossible and resources are scarce). The entire length of this wall is littered with antipersonnel mines to discourage people from moving freely across.

This is, in itself, a violation of a basic human right described in both the Universal Charter on Human Rights (United Nations) and the Charter on Human and Peoples' Rights (African Union): the right to move freely. Furthermore, the colonization of the SADR by Morocco violates Article 20 (1) of the African Charter, which states, "All peoples shall have the right to existence. They shall have the unquestionable and inalienable right to self-determination. They shall freely determine their political status and shall pursue their economic and social development according to the policy they have freely chosen."

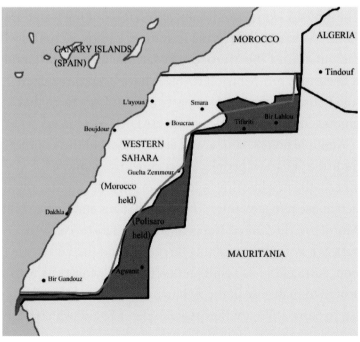

A different understanding of boundaries: Morocco-controlled Western Sahara is in yellow, and the Polisario-controlled territory is in orange. The pink line shows the wall Morocco built.

In addition, the African Charter on Human and Peoples' Rights recognizes that not only individuals, but people groups as a collective, are entitled to "the peoples' rights to **development**, free disposal of natural resources, and self-determination."

In the absence of the Saharawi peoples' right to self-determination, to development, and to choose how to dispose of their natural resources, the people have been made vulnerable to additional violations. According to the Office of the UN High Commissioner for Human Rights (OHCHR), "Almost all human rights violations in Western Sahara stem from the non-implementation of the Saharawi people's fundamental right to self-determination." For instance, Saharawi people are unable to earn their own livelihoods, relying on humanitarian aid groups to meet their basic needs. Yet health care, food, sanitation, and safe drinking water are difficult to obtain while living in refugee camps. Activists who speak out against the Moroccan government risk arrest, and in a few cases, pro-Moroccan voices have been threatened by the Polisario (the political party and military force that promotes the independence of the SADR).

Multiple points of view and stakeholders in this conflict include the Saharawi people; the occupying country of Morocco; the neighboring countries of Algeria and Mauritania, which house refugee camps; the United States and France (allies of Morocco); the United Nations (which refers to Western Sahara as a non-self-governing territory); and the European Union, particularly its fishing industry, which contracts with Morocco to make use of the rich natural resources found in Western Sahara. Yet another stakeholder is Spain, which hosts Saharawi refugee children during the hottest, driest seasons and has given some of these children Spanish citizenship once they became adults and permanently emigrated.

Morocco

In terms of human rights, Morocco's record is mixed. On one hand, its treatment of the Saharawi people and their territory has led to a deplorable situation in which hundreds of thousands of Saharawi refugees have been forced to live in semipermanent camps in the neighboring countries of Algeria and Mauritania—and this has been going on for almost forty years. This means that two generations of people have grown up in refugee camps, while Morocco and the Polisario have yet to reach an acceptable agreement. Imagine being born in a refugee camp and living there until age forty, bringing up your children there and not knowing how much longer it will be before the future will be stable.

On the other hand, Morocco's new and improved 2011 constitution provides a path toward democracy for its citizens, recognition and respect for the plurality of its identity (representing many tribes, languages, religions, and ethnicities), a stronger notion of gender equality than it has had in the past, a list of rights and freedoms rooted in universal standards of human rights, separation of powers, a strong judicial authority, and a territorial democracy (regionalization), along with specific principles of good governance, ethical standards for public life, and protection for private property.

Algeria

A question we can ask ourselves while considering northern Africa in particular is, "What is the relationship between human rights and the war on terror?" Often, overzealous governments take an extreme approach when attempting to combat terror and end up oppressing their own people and compromising their ideals of human rights. Algeria is a case in point. In the 1990s, due to fears over terrorism, the government declared a state of emergency that continued for nineteen years. More specifically, because it appeared that an **Islamist** group would be elected to office, elections were canceled and the military took control. Under this state of emergency, the government placed severe restrictions on the press, religion, personal liberties, travel, and many other aspects of ordinary life. For instance, some Catholic and Protestant groups were not allowed to import Christian literature. All media had to obtain approval for all publications.

Since then, however, Algeria has made great strides in expanding freedoms and increasing respect for human rights. For example, in February 2011, the state of emergency was lifted. Torture has been criminalized, and protections for detainees in police custody are strictly regulated by the Criminal Code. Algeria has also launched a national plan called "Algeria Worthy of its Children," aimed to "provide a better life, to guarantee quality education, and better protect children from abuse, exploitation and violence." Unfortunately, human trafficking, including that of children, continues in spite of legislation forbidding it.

For women, Algeria has taken actions to encourage greater participation in public life. As of 2014, women held 31 percent of the seats in the new assembly. (Compare this figure to that of the United States Congress, where, as of 2015, women comprised 20 percent of the Senate and only 19.3 percent of the House of Representatives.) Recently, the women of Algeria were given permission to travel with their children without obtaining their husband's formal consent (men have never faced similar restrictions).

It is also worth noting that Algeria abolished the death penalty in 1993, although the death sentence is still pronounced in courts (but not carried out).

Mauritania

The greatest obstacle facing Mauritania as it moves toward greater democracy is its long history of racial and ethnic discrimination, which is embedded in its traditional practices of slavery and the caste system.

In addition, women do not have equality with men. According to a 2014 report by the United Nations Committee on Elimination of Discrimination Against Women, **nongovernmental organizations (NGOs)** from Mauritania have reported that women face "problems such as rape, kidnapping, trafficking, domestic violence, early marriage, and **female genital mutilation/cutting (FGM/C)**. Mauritania has a high rate of maternal mortality, the highest in the sub-region at 626 deaths per 100,000 live births." The report also mentioned that slavery was still practiced in urban areas. Mauritania demonstrates "inequalities between women and men." Other problems include early marriage, child marriage, and polygamy.

On the bright side, however, in 2009 Mauritania agreed to welcome human rights monitoring by the United Nations, indicating its willingness to hear feedback and evaluate and address these problems.

The Arab Spring: Tunisia, Egypt, and Libya

Human rights across northern Africa are deeply affected by the political frameworks at play. In 2011, Tunisia's Jasmine Revolution inspired similar revolutions in Egypt, Libya, and elsewhere. The series of revolutions is called, collectively, the Arab Spring and is significant in that it was the first time that social media platforms such as Twitter played a strong role in revolution.

Tunisian protesters in the early days of the Arab Spring, in January 2011, in Tunis

It was also the first time since 1979 that revolution was successful in a northern African or Middle Eastern country. With revolutions, however, comes instability. Therefore, it's common for revolutions to lead to unlawful activities such as the trafficking of guns, drugs, and people.

Tunisia

Because of the role of social media in Tunisia's Jasmine Revolution, people throughout the world were able to track events on the ground, in real time. Humanitarian groups and activists, and people of all ages, especially youth, were able to organize themselves and communicate through 140-character tweets that helped with logistics. For example, some tweets invited volunteers to donate blood or assist at a hospital, others warned of snipers' gunfire at the African Development Bank or asked for help and received it promptly from their Twitter followers. Protests were planned and organized through social media. One tweet read, "Tomorrow: 1 million Tunisian will strike peacefully in av Habib Bourguiba downtown."

The government responded by shutting down Twitter, but global citizens outside Tunisia allowed their IP addresses to host activists' Twitter accounts in order to allow the revolutionaries to work around censorship. Since then, Tunisia has ratified a new constitution, has elected a new president, and is enjoying the benefits of a relatively (though not entirely) peaceful revolution.

Egypt

Egypt's revolution of 2011 is called the 25 January Revolution, a peaceful popular revolution against the ruling regime, which was said to be politically and financially corrupt. Egyptians demanded respect for their rights and liberties. Unfortunately, the next president elected implemented tyrannical measures, threatening the rule of law and vying for greater power for his party, the Muslim Brotherhood. This president's actions divided the Egyptian people, pitting religious groups against one another, even though Egypt has had a long history of welcoming both Muslims and Christians, as well as other religious minorities, to participate in the political process. In 2013, a second revolution happened, ousting the regime. A new constitution was put to a **referendum** (a vote on a particular issue) and approved by a 98 percent majority. The amended constitution was adopted in 2014, a victory for the revolution and for human rights as it devoted a whole chapter to the protection of rights and freedoms for its people.

Under the current leadership of President Abdel Fattah el-Sisi, the focus has been on stabilizing the region—at the expense of freedom of speech. Because the Muslim

Brotherhood had funded newspapers to spread rumors and provoke further revolution, Egypt responded by diminishing the freedom of the press. Since August 2015, an antiterrorism law designed in the interest of national security forbids journalists from reporting any nonofficial versions of terrorist attacks.

For Christians, there is some discrimination but they consider the current president the best that has come to leadership in the history of Egypt. For example, President Sisi attended church on Christmas; this was the first time an Egyptian president had done this (the official religion of Egypt is Islam). Some of the current administration is left over from the old regime, however, and they benefit from the status quo, which included tension between Christians and Muslims.

In 2016, in response to increased threats from encroaching terrorist groups from neighboring countries like Sudan and Libya, Egyptians have seen stricter government control over assemblies and protests, along with decreased freedoms of speech and the press. Increased tension between Muslims and Christians was shown in June 2016 when a mob captured an elderly Christian woman whose son was dating a Muslim woman and paraded the woman naked through the neighborhood. Events like this show that progress happens not once and for all, but in fits and starts, with backward steps as well as forward ones.

Libya

The story of Libya's revolution does not have a happy ending—at least not yet. In 2011, as the Arab Spring was in full swing, Libyans rose up to remove their leader of forty-plus years, Muammar Gaddafi (you might also see his name spelled Qaddafi or other variations—it has more than 112 spellings), but in the absence of a secure government to

Waterfront promenade in Benghazi, Libya, in January 2004, before the revolution (*above*); compare to Laithi district, in Benghazi, in 2016 after violent revolution and its aftermath (*below*)

fill the void left by the long dictatorship, the country has devolved into civil war with no end in sight.

At one point in 2014, more than 1,700 different armed groups were fighting each other in Libya. With so many factions, it has been virtually impossible to create a stable structure that represents all Libyans. Mass crimes abound, including widespread killing, rapes, destruction of entire villages, and deportations. Five years after Gaddafi's fall, trust in the nation's weak government institutions is extremely low. Political elites, unable to agree on a new government structure, continue to deploy armed militias. In the face of chaos and destruction, human rights violations are rampant, and there are no legal institutions strong and trusted enough to serve justice.

Extremist groups such as the Islamic State (ISIS, also called Daesh or ISIL) and Ansar al-Sharia terrorize citizens,

Vestiges of Colonialism

During nineteenth- and early-twentieth-century colonialism, Egypt was a British colony. Libya was occupied by Italy, and Tunisia was a French colony. Each colonial power influenced its respective colony's legal system, social structure, and official language. These legacies remain. Libyans, upon greeting their friends, kiss them once on each cheek, in the Italian fashion. Many educated Libyans can read Italian, and their legal system consists of a mixture of traditional tribal law and Italian law. Tunisians today typically speak their own dialect, standard Arabic, and French. In Egypt, although the official language is standard Arabic, the native language is an Egyptian dialect that includes nine thousand Coptic words, with fragments of English and French mixed in. Most educated Egyptians also speak English, French, and other languages.

Prior to being a British colony, Egypt had also been conquered at various points in history by Turkey, Israel, the Ottoman Empire, and others. During the recent revolutions, a joke was frequently posted on Twitter and Facebook: "When we study history in school, there is a lot to study—too many wars and occupations. When we had the revolution, we wanted to put an end to having more of this so that the next generation would not have so much to study!" This is one example of how the revolution made use of social media, where activists could garner support and also express themselves through humor.

persecuting anyone who disagrees with them. Their methods include assassinations, disappearances, detentions, torture—even death by crucifixion.

Many attempts have been made to forge a unified government, but it will take a long time to rebuild a strong civil society in Libya. In the meantime, there is little security for ordinary citizens. Very few NGOs are willing to take the risks; Human Rights Watch is reporting on a limited basis, but it must be done in secret. Therefore, human rights violations in today's Libya are greatly underreported.

Without a societal structure to provide a mechanism for justice, some people take the law into their own hands, reinforcing extremism and continuing a perpetual cycle of violence. But as Libyan peace-building practitioner Najla El Mangoush has said, "When you fight against extremism, who are you fighting? Is 'extremism' your neighbor?" In other words, violence cannot be ended by violence.

Northern African Human Rights in Context

North Americans and others in the global economy are connected to northern Africa because many nations rely on its natural resources. Human rights abuses, particularly trafficking in persons, link northern Africa to other countries that participate in illegal markets. It is impossible to remain isolated from the issues that northern Africa faces today. The international community has a powerful role to play in a variety of contexts, including the United Nations, the United States Institute of Peace, human rights–based organizations, military or peacekeeping actions, economic markets, and in speaking out on behalf of human and peoples' rights for citizens and refugees in northern Africa.

This woman in the northeast part of Nigeria has scars on her cheeks that are traditional markings that indicate her tribe.

2 Western Africa

ccording to the African Union's designations, western Africa consists of the following countries: Benin, Burkina Faso, Cabo Verde (or Cape Verde), Côte d'Ivoire (or Ivory Coast), the Gambia, Ghana, Guinea, Guinea-Bissau, Liberia, Mali, Niger, Nigeria, Senegal, Sierra Leone, and Togo. It is worth noting that some of these countries have similar-sounding names. Guinea and Guinea-Bissau are different countries, and neither should be confused with Equatorial Guinea (covered in chapter 3 as part of central Africa). Furthermore, all three of these "Guineas" should be distinguished from New Guinea and Papua New Guinea—neither of which are located on the African continent! Niger and Nigeria, too, sound similar but are neighbors. The local people pronounce Niger the French way ("Nee-jzhair" with a very soft *g* sound) because it was formerly a French colony, and Nigeria is usually pronounced with a British accent due to its former status as a British colony.

Since it is not possible to cover all fifteen of the western African countries thoroughly, this chapter will present an overview of some the most important human rights issues facing the region as a whole, then focus on one country in greater detail; Nigeria is particularly interesting to study because of its complexity. In some ways, Nigeria has made tremendous strides for human rights, yet it has a long journey ahead in other ways.

The UN and the OHCHR

The UN Office of the High Commissioner for Human Rights (OHCHR) has identified the following as the greatest problems to be addressed in western Africa:

- Impunity, including in particular as it relates to widespread sexual and **gender-based violence** in the sub-region;

- Trafficking in persons;

- Human rights and elections;

- Economic, cultural, and social rights, including the human rights implications of poverty, migration, and climate change;

- Human rights in security sector reform (SSR).

Impunity

What is **impunity**? The word refers to a situation where crimes have clearly been committed, but the justice system fails to adequately address them. Widespread impunity is bad for a stable society because it not only allows wrong behavior to continue, it also causes people to distrust the justice system (which can cause them to take justice into their own hands). A government that tolerates impunity often loses credibility with its people.

A historical example of impunity in western Africa occurred during Guinea's first decades of independence from France. In 1958, Sekou Touré became dictator and remained in power for the rest of his life (more than thirty years). He killed people who opposed him, and his spies were widespread. Guinea is a tiny country with every necessary resource. It also has precious metals and diamonds. But Touré did not use the profits from Guinea's resources for human development or growth; instead, he kept the wealth for himself and for his friends. During his rule, many Guineans fled the country for a better life in neighboring Côte d'Ivoire or elsewhere. Even after his death, people were still so frightened that they would close all the doors and windows before speaking about him. He was never caught or tried in a court of law. This is impunity.

A more recent example is in the Gambia, ruled by a dictator name Yahya Jammeh who ousted the previous leader in a 1994 coup and has remained in power since. Human rights groups have long accused the Gambian government of harassing activists and journalists. In 2004, a new law allowed for journalists to be jailed for libel and sedition. A critic of the law, Deyda Hydara, was shot dead days later. Other journalists have disappeared or been imprisoned. In 2009, Jammeh threatened to kill human rights workers. Jammeh has yet to face justice.

Gender-Based Violence

In Senegal, gender-based violence is commonly accepted. For example, in a 2012 survey, 60 percent of women in one region of Senegal thought it was acceptable for a husband to commit domestic violence for reasons like "burning food, going out without telling him, neglecting children, or for refusing sex." Even though Senegal's constitution guarantees equality between men and women and Senegal has signed on to international agreements to protect women from violence, women in this country still experience high rates of violence.

Another form of gender-based violence prevalent not only in western Africa, but also in central and eastern Africa, is female genital mutilation/cutting (FGM/C). Because of cultural beliefs, various forms of FGM/C are practiced in twenty-nine African countries (in spite of its illegality in some countries). Much like circumcision for males, many believe the practice is a hygienic one (though FGM/C often means the removal of an extensive portion of a woman's or girl's external genitalia). Other reasons for the practice, which traces back centuries, are related to views about sexuality. It causes serious short-term and long-term health problems, including difficulties with menstruation, urinary tract infections, and higher rates of maternal and/or infant death during childbirth.

According to UNICEF, 97 percent of females ages fifteen to forty-nine in Guinea have experienced this procedure. Female circumcision is not restricted to a particular ethnic group or religion; it is practiced by Muslims, Christians, and traditional African religions alike. The United Nations, however, considers FGM/C to be a form of gender-based violence and is trying to combat this practice. Some former practitioners of FGM/C (the older women who perform the ritual) have stopped the practice after they were taught about the health risks. These women now speak out against the practice, raising awareness in their own cultures. This demonstrates how proper education can be very successful in reducing gender-related violence and other human rights violations. Many human rights and health-related organizations are working to reduce the prevalence of FGM/C worldwide since the practice also occurs in parts of the Middle East, in Asia, and in places where immigrants from these countries settle, such as Europe and the United States.

Trafficking in Persons

Although slavery has been made illegal in every country (most recently in Niger in 2003 and Mauritania in 2007), slavery and trafficking in persons still continues. Sometimes slavery is practiced according to social class or skin color, especially in Mauritania (where 10 to 20 percent of the population is illegally enslaved, according to the human rights group Anti-Slavery International) and in Niger and Mali, where slavery exists in a sort of caste system. Other times people fall into the condition through debt bondage, sexual slavery, and child slavery.

Because slavery is illegal everywhere, some governments deny it exists, and antislavery activists in western Africa have been arrested and tortured. Journalists who report on it have been jailed or evicted from the country. Part of the problem with ending slavery is that those who are enslaved are often not aware that it is wrong; they believe that it is their lot by birth.

Human Rights and Elections

A sad reality in many parts of Africa is that elections often bring greater human rights violations than at ordinary times. This is partly because democracy is still a relatively new concept for African nations, most of which have earned their independence as recently as the 1960s. It naturally takes time for people and cultures to adapt to a brand-new style of governance, especially in regions that have been disrupted by power-hungry dictators who refuse to acknowledge term limits or by intertribal conflicts that interfere with fair processes.

Some of the western African countries that have especially suffered in this way in recent history are Liberia, Sierra Leone, Côte d'Ivoire, and Guinea. In these countries, some elections have led to civil war instead of peaceful democracy.

Economic, Cultural, and Social Rights

Three special challenges when it comes to protecting the economic, cultural, and social rights of west Africans are

Among the Tuareg, it is the men who cover their faces from the age of puberty, while women's faces are shown.

poverty, migration, and climate change. These factors work together in a feedback loop so that poverty sometimes leads to migration, climate change leads to both poverty and migration, and all three of these interrelated factors present challenges for human rights. For example, if a tribe or clan is forced to migrate to a new region due to climate change, they may face discrimination by their new neighbors. Poverty can be caused by climate (such as drought, flooding, famine, and natural disaster), but it can also be caused by lack of opportunity in a new social setting due to discrimination or lack of protection. People who are displaced may be forced to give up some of their cultural or social identity as they adapt to a new environment.

Human Rights and the Security Sector

In western Africa (and elsewhere), security forces (such as police) and others employed to protect people sometimes end up violating human rights. This can happen through excessive force, torture, disappearances, and **extrajudicial killings**— that is, when people accused of a crime are put to death outside of the legal system, without trial or due process. The causes of security abuses include inadequate training in how to appropriately keep the peace and the problem of low wages, which leads to corruption and the acceptance of bribes. In countries where police are not paid in a timely or regular manner, they may even rely on favors or bribes to provide for their families. Another factor is lack of accountability; when police and security forces are not called to account for the crimes they commit, such actions are likely to continue.

Providing better training and adequate resources to police and other security personnel has been very effective in reducing human rights violations toward citizens. Additionally, a justice system that punishes offenders and does not turn a blind eye toward corruption and excessive force deters this type of behavior.

Ghana is an example of a western African nation where a free press helps to draw attention to violations by police and bring them to justice.

ECOWAS

The Economic Community of West African States (ECOWAS) is another organization that promotes human rights. Although its primary purpose is to improve the economic situation of western Africa, ECOWAS recognizes that promoting human rights is directly related to improving an economy. Unlike the OHCHR, ECOWAS is an African group; it includes fifteen western African countries. These countries joined together in 1975 to overcome the isolation they experienced after independence from colonialism. According to ECOWAS itself, the group's purpose is to promote cooperation in economic activities including "industry, transport, telecommunications, energy, agriculture, natural resources, commerce, monetary and financial questions, social and cultural matters." It is also active in promoting human and peoples' rights—its treaty guarantees its people the provisions stated in the African Charter on Human and Peoples' Rights.

The ECOWAS website identifies the following important points of focus: economic development for women, community development, economic partnerships, conflict prevention, education, and elections observations.

Interestingly, when one compares the wording of the UN's OHCHR report with the wording from ECOWAS, it is apparent that the African organization frames the issues quite differently from the UN. For example, while the UN discusses the problem of "sexual and gender-based violence," ECOWAS's organization includes a Gender Development Centre.

ECOWAS has taken on a human rights role since it began accepting individual complaints for human rights violations in 2005. It also actively supports young people, as shown through its "Declaration on the Decade of a Culture of the Rights of the Child in West Africa" (2001–2010). ECOWAS recognizes the powerful roles that young people and women can play in western Africa's development as they work together to solve problems, reduce poverty, and create more options for its people.

Poverty and Lack of Human Development

Some western African countries have unusually low life expectancies compared to global statistics. For instance, according to the World Health Organization (WHO), the global average life expectancy is 71.4. In Burkina Faso, however, life expectancy from birth is only 52 years. In Côte d'Ivoire, it is 53, and in Sierra Leone, it is just 50 years.

How Does One Measure Human Development?

The Human Development Index (HDI) is intended to measure the quality of human life apart from simply looking at economic statistics. Countries that rank high on the HDI have excellent quality education, access to health care, meaningful work, and opportunities to contribute to culture, participate in politics and governance, and develop meaningful lives. According to the 2015 HDI rankings, the top ten countries were Norway, Australia, Switzerland, Denmark, Netherlands, Germany, Ireland, United States, Canada, and New Zealand. No African countries were included in the "Very High Human Development" section, although three were considered to have "High" development: Mauritius, and perhaps surprisingly, Libya and Tunisia—in spite of their recent revolutions and the current crisis in Libya.

African countries that have "medium" development include: Egypt, Gabon, Cabo Verde, Morocco, Namibia, Congo, Equatorial Guinea, Zambia, Ghana, and São Tomé and Príncipe (these countries are sprinkled throughout various subregions, including northern, western, central, and southern Africa, but none in eastern Africa).

The remaining African countries score "low" in human development: Kenya, Swaziland, Tanzania, Nigeria, Cameroon, Madagascar, Zimbabwe, Mauritania, Comoros, Lesotho, Togo, Rwanda, Uganda, Benin, Sudan, Djibouti, South Sudan, Senegal, Côte d'Ivoire, Malawi, Ethiopia, Gambia, DR Congo, Liberia, Guinea-Bissau, Mali, Mozambique, Sierra Leone, Guinea, Burkina Faso, Burundi, Chad, Eritrea, Central African Republic, and Niger, which ranked last. (Data was not available for Somalia.)

Some of the factors reducing life expectancy are poverty (about half of the population of western Africa lives below the poverty level), infectious diseases from lack of sanitation and clean water, HIV/AIDS, and a high rate of infant mortality as well as maternal mortality (death in childbirth).

Another interesting consideration to think about is median age. In the United States, according to the *CIA World Factbook*, the median age is 37—meaning half the population is older than 37 and half is younger. The country with the lowest median age is Niger, at 15. This may explain why Niger ranks last in human development—most of its people are too young to have reached their potential.

Extremist Groups and Terrorism

Poverty and lack of development in western Africa make people vulnerable to extremist terrorist groups. Such groups promise to provide security and basic needs when the government has failed to provide them.

People who are unemployed and have few economic opportunities are at risk for being recruited by terrorist organizations. This is why extremist militant groups such as al-Qaeda, Al-Shabaab, the Islamic State (also called Daesh, or ISIL/ISIS), and others have been able to grow and expand in countries where economic instability and high rates of unemployment are problematic. These include Mali, Nigeria, Niger, Burkina Faso, and some of the northern African countries previously discussed. Cameroon and Chad (in central Africa) are also presently vulnerable to these groups, as well as most eastern African countries including Kenya, Somalia, Sudan, Uganda, and Eritrea. Across the Sahel region, drought contributes to water and food scarcity, putting people especially at risk.

Arbitrary National Boundaries

The influence colonialism and imperialism have had on the countries of Africa is wide-reaching—so much so as to have shaped national boundaries, often without regard for where particular ethnic groups or tribes lived. In some areas, particular tribes were chosen by colonialists to rule over others, which created long-standing animosity that would later erupt into civil war and even **genocide**.

Neocolonialism is a word that describes how Western influences continue to affect Africa even after colonialism ended. For instance, the World Bank is run by Western countries and exerts considerable influence over African states. Western countries influence former colonies through media, business/enterprise, and "good intentions." Although African countries are politically independent, their economies are tied to the West.

Unemployment can stir of up feelings of rage, discontent, and hopelessness, which militant groups play on. In turn, the resulting conflicts further destroy both lives and livelihoods, reducing the capacity to find legitimate, productive work. Migrants and refugees are more susceptible due to their poverty status and higher rates of discrimination by potential employers. The vicious cycle repeats itself as a less stable society produces less ability to find stable livelihoods and desperate people turn to desperate causes.

This is one reason why groups including the OHCHR, the Danish Institute for Human Rights, the UN, and ECOWAS emphasize **sustainable development** to create alternative options for people living in poverty.

Rights for Children

Children everywhere are among the most vulnerable people because they are small, not fully educated, unable to vote, and virtually powerless. The United Nations created a legal protection called the Convention on the Rights of the Child, and the African Union decided to elaborate on that with the African Committee on the Rights and Welfare of the Child.

Both of these documents intend to protect children's rights through "non-discrimination, participation, the best interests of the child, and survival and development." The African version provides a few extra features to suit its context, with additional statements to protect children living in apartheid, to protect girls from harmful practices (such as FGM/C or forced marriage), to address children in regions with internal conflict and displacement, to clarify the definition of a child, to protect children of imprisoned mothers and those living in poor and unsanitary conditions, and to elaborate on children's responsibilities to their families and communities.

Boko Haram

In April 2014, the Islamist militant group Boko Haram kidnapped 276 schoolgirls from their secondary school in Chibok, Nigeria. Boko Haram promotes a version of Islam that forbids Muslims to take part in any political or social activity

Family and friends protest in hopes the Nigerian government will do more to rescue the kidnapped Chibok schoolgirls who have been missing since 2014.

associated with Western society. Most Muslims worldwide strongly oppose such Islamist extremists, believing instead that the true Islam is peaceful (*Islam* means "peace" in Arabic.)

Boko Haram plans to establish a caliphate (an independent Islamist state), independent of Nigeria, that would function in farming and trading, apart from modern civilization. It has joined the Islamic State. In the past seven years, its actions have killed more than fifteen thousand people and displaced two million more in Nigeria, Chad, Niger, and Cameroon.

In addition to the Chibok schoolgirls, many other children have been killed, forcibly enslaved, or married. Those who manage to return to their families often face stigma because of their involvement with Boko Haram and are sometimes rejected by their communities.

In May 2016, one of the Chibok girls was found and returned to her home. Nigerian president Buhari met her and her four-month-old son and promised them education and health care.

In May 2016, two years after the Chibok kidnapping, one of the girls was found and returned to her family. By then, she had an infant son. President Muhammadu Buhari of Nigeria (elected after the kidnapping) welcomed her back and promised to provide for her and her son's health and education. President Buhari has also initiated a massive attempt to improve education in the north of the country in an attempt to alleviate the chronic poverty in that area.

Case Study on Human Rights: Nigeria

Much could be written about human rights in western Africa, but it is worthwhile to focus on a single country to get a comprehensive sense of the many factors at play. Nigeria is an example worthy of a closer look. Nigeria's constitution and its National Commission on Human Rights demonstrate Nigeria's intentions to improve human rights within its borders. In other ways, Nigeria still faces numerous challenges because of the wide gulf between the rich and the poor, severe corruption at all levels of governance, and militant extremism in the north.

Nigeria is rich in oil and other natural resources, which is both a blessing and a curse. Because of its richness, it was badly exploited as a British colony, and today, its people are still exploited through trade agreements that benefit only its wealthiest citizens. The poor in Nigeria do not receive compensation for their country's treasure trove of resources: public services are chronically underfunded. In 2013, Transparency International, an organization that measures ethics in all of the world's countries to try to hold them accountable, ranked Nigeria 144 out of 170 because of its high level of corruption in the public sector. While there is plenty of wealth in the nation, provision for public goods like education, police protection, and infrastructure are inadequate.

As for many African countries, the roots of some of these problems can be traced to colonialism. For example, in the past, the British colonial government refused to allow Christian missionaries to build schools in northern Nigeria; today, the region has a high rate of illiteracy, a low rate of education, high poverty, and other factors that feed into extremism. In the northeastern part of Nigeria, without proper schools, children are sent to local imams for a Koran-based education but not provided with food and shelter. During the hours when they are not being taught, they wander the streets seeking their basic needs. This feeds into the cycle of poverty.

Nigeria is the most populous African country, with a great diversity of tribes and more than five hundred languages. This can be described as a form of wealth (in human capital and culture), but the flip side is that so much diversity can lead to conflict. The Biafran War is the name Nigerians gave to their civil war, which pitted the three major tribes (Igbo, Yoruba, and Hausa) against one another in 1967. Additional minority tribes were drawn in. Author Chinua Achebe described that time in his novel *Things Fall Apart*. Today the nation has largely recovered from the Biafran War, but traces remain. Many people remember the strong feelings of tension between different tribes and ethnic groups as they struggled to redistribute the balance of power.

Contemporary Nigeria has worked diligently to create good laws, but implementing them brings challenges. For example, according to the 1999 Nigerian Constitution, a person who is arrested should be charged in court within forty-eight hours. The law states that the police should let the suspect know, in the language that he understands, why he has been arrested. The problem is that so many languages are spoken in Nigeria. If someone from a minority ethnic group is arrested and does not speak English (the official language) or the other most common ones (Igbo, Yoruba, and Hausa), the police struggle to communicate with him. Yet a vital part of promoting cultural and social rights includes preserving indigenous and local languages because they are essential to maintaining a tribe's unique identity. This example illustrates how different aspects of human rights sometimes exist in tension with one another.

Western African Human Rights in Context

Issues that affect western African countries also affect the global community, especially as militant extremist organizations threaten and attack nations abroad. Global

The Great Mosque of Djenne in Mali features elaborate details such as minarets.

trade, mainly the export of oil, ties western Africa to the West. No one can forget how the Ebola epidemic, which started in western Africa, began to affect people throughout the world. Ebola would likely have become much worse if not for international health care workers and organizations who did their part to stem the spread of disease.

The international community has an excellent opportunity to continue partnering with organizations deeply connected to the grassroots levels in western Africa to improve the lives of women and children, to improve opportunities for human and economic development, and to create a better story than the historic ones of slavery and colonialism.

The best chance for a bright future for children in central Africa is a good education.

3 | Central Africa

T he African Union designates the following countries as central African nations: Burundi, Cameroon, Central African Republic (CAR), Chad, Republic of Congo (often called simply "Congo"), Democratic Republic of Congo (DR Congo), Equatorial Guinea, Gabon, and São Tomé and Príncipe. Congo and DR Congo are commonly confused with one another but are actually neighboring countries with separate governments. Interestingly, São Tomé and Príncipe is not located directly on the continent but rather consists of a series of islands nearby.

As in most of Africa, religions in central Africa include Islam, Christianity, and indigenous **animistic** beliefs. Some conflicts and human rights issues relate to clashes between different religious groups, but most violence is motivated by ethnic or political differences rather than religion. Conflicts frequently arise between the differing lifestyles and land use by nomadic, herding peoples and those who are settled and rely on agriculture. The settled people do not appreciate herds of roaming cattle eating their crops, while the herders wish to continue their tradition of migrating according to seasonal patterns and the availability of water, seeing assimilation into developing culture as a betrayal of their identity.

Human rights issues pervade virtually all of central Africa, including inhumane prison conditions, oppressive governments, excessive use of force by police and other security forces, lack of a strong justice system, and discrimination and violence against women and children. Refugees fleeing conflicts in eastern Africa find their way into DR Congo and Central Africa Republic, countries that are already beset by conflicts of their own. The "African world war" took place here, which is how many refer to the Second Congo War because it involved parties from nine African countries.

Burundi

Burundi is one of three African nations of special concern to the United Nations, along with Central African Republic (CAR) and Democratic Republic of Congo (DR Congo).

According to the United States Bureau of Democracy, Human Rights, and Labor, Burundi's main human rights abuses in 2015 included extrajudicial killings with victims buried in mass graves, arbitrary arrests often for political reasons, imprisoning people under inhumane and life-threatening conditions, and widespread oppression of freedoms of speech, press and media, assembly, and association. Amnesty International (AI) released a report in January 2016 showing satellite imagery of mass graves. Government corruption is also a problem.

Women and girls face widespread gender-based violence and discrimination. Other groups that face discrimination include people with albinism (little to no pigment in their skin and hair), people with disabilities, and LGBTI people. Impunity is a serious problem in this country.

Police are vulnerable to corruption and bribery because they are poorly paid and poorly trained, and 75 percent of

The East African Court of Justice (EACJ)

T he **East African Court of Justice** includes Burundi, Kenya, Rwanda, Uganda, and Tanzania. Its purpose is to interpret cases that relate to "the rule of law." Founded in 2001, the EACJ heard its first case in 2005. In a 2007 case, the court made a decision indicating that it may consider cases that include human rights as a component despite the fact that its authority is limited to cases pertaining to "rule of law." This limit has been expanded to include human rights cases if, and only if, the case includes a violation of law. As summarized by Open Society Foundations lawyers, the court in this case found "that the overriding consideration of the rule of law is that both the rulers and the governed are equally subject to the same law of the land." Therefore, if (in this case) the Ugandan "armed security agents violated the principle of the rule of law," then the court could hear the case involving human rights violations against Ugandan people who were affected. Since that case, the EACJ has heard a number of additional cases that involved human rights violations as long as they fit within the context of the rule of law. Significantly, in 2016, the president of the EACJ attended an international meeting in Brazil called the 2016 World Environmental Law Congress. The EACJ recognizes that as global climate change affects people in African nations, more laws will be needed to protect people from injustices related to environmental issues. Environmental rule of law is a growing and developing field that is likely to become more important in the future.

them are former rebels, according to the United States State Department. Partly because of their lack of proper training, police prevent citizens from exercising civil rights and have been known to torture and to kill. In April and May of 2015, police were so brutal in response to civilian protests that the military had to intervene. The government has been slow to investigate and prosecute.

Cameroon

According to the 2015 report by the United States Bureau of Democracy, Human Rights and Labor on Cameroon, the significant issues in Cameroon were Boko Haram killings in the far north region, the use of child soldiers, abductions, beheadings, and immolations. Boko Haram has killed hundreds of civilians.

In response, Cameroon security forces (such as police) retaliated against Boko Haram suspects with torture and abuse, denying the right to trial, and imprisoning them in life-threatening conditions. In makeshift jail cells, detainees have died of suffocation and from toxic gases. Prisoners are provided only one meal per day; the budget for food in prisons was only 43 cents per day per prisoner in 2014. Prisons are so overcrowded that they hold as many as four to five times the intended capacity. In one example, twenty-two prisoners were held overnight in a 40-square-foot (3.7-square-meter) cell, where one of them died of suffocation. In such crowded and inadequate conditions, illness spreads: malnutrition, tuberculosis, and bronchitis, along with infections, parasites, dehydration, and diarrhea are all threats. To make matters worse, some of these prisoners are innocent citizens who have been arrested arbitrarily; some are held for years without being charged with a crime and some are even children. Furthermore, the Cameroon government has seized private property, conducted secret trials of Boko Haram suspects, and restricted freedoms of speech and the press, as well as freedom of movement. Even though these rights are protected under the constitution, other laws criminalize media offenses, such as criticizing government policy.

Other human rights problems in this country include gender-based violence such as female genital mutilation/ cutting (FGM/C), human trafficking, and discrimination toward the minority group called the Mbororo. Unfortunately, many times these violations are met with impunity.

Human Rights for Women in Cameroon

A less common human rights issue in Cameroon is that of widow rites, still practiced in the southern region. When a woman is widowed, her family forces her to shave all her hair from her body and forego hygiene for an extended period of time. Sometimes widows are forcibly married to a relative of their deceased husband. Women are legally provided equality with men, but because of customary practices, such laws are not always followed. For example, in some ethnic groups, women are not allowed to inherit property; therefore, after a woman's husband dies, the family's land is given to someone else. On the positive side, the Cameroon government has taken steps to educate and to reduce the practice of FGM/C, which is considered one of the greatest human rights issues for African women.

Human Rights for Children in Cameroon

Primary education is compulsory for children, but no particular age is set; generally, children complete school around age twelve or thirteen. School is unaffordable for many children due to uniforms, books, and other fees. Unregistered Quranic schools have been found to have illegal prisons where children and adults are chained, starved, and tortured. Children have reportedly been left there by parents who did not know how to handle their behavioral problems or mental disabilities. Child abuse is common in Cameroon, with 76 percent of children reporting that they were frequently hit at home. The AU Charter on the Rights and Welfare of the Child aims to formally address these issues.

Central African Republic

The Central African Republic has been unstable since it became independent from France in 1960. In January 2014, Catherine Samba Panza was elected interim president of a transitional government. Armed groups still control territories throughout the country, however, acting as governing institutions, taxing people, providing security, and appointing leaders. One such group is the notorious Lord's Resistance Army (LRA) started in Uganda. Others include rebel groups that support former leaders that have been removed from power, a group called Revolution and Justice, and the Democratic Front of the Central African People.

While the situation has improved since 2014, the whole population is still at risk. Serious violations of international human rights continue to occur, including disappearances, torture, rape, and the use of child soldiers. Forced labor and human trafficking are also problematic. Children are sometimes forced into domestic servitude, prostitution, agricultural labor, mining, and other work not of their own choosing. A fact that reveals the difficulty of life in this country is life expectancy, which is about fifty years.

On the other hand, the United Nations has established a National Committee for Genocide Prevention in this country. The committee works at "both national and regional levels to prevent genocide, war crimes and crimes against humanity." This committee highlights both the extreme level of risk in this country as well as the role the international community can take to mitigate those risks.

Chad

Chad has one of the lowest life expectancy rates in the world (49 years for men and 52 years for women, according to the *CIA World Factbook*). Compare this to the global average life expectancy of 71.4 years, according to the World Health Organization in 2015.

A river forms the border between the DR Congo and CAR, where violent conflict has disrupted life. This nun and imam have spent many years promoting peace between their communities.

Chad is a semidesert country but rich in gold, uranium, and oil. Since its independence from France in 1960, the country has been fraught with instability and violence, mostly stemming from tension between the Arab-Muslim north and the Christian and animist south. In 2003, Chad became an oil exporter with a pipeline connecting it to Cameroon. Unfortunately, in 2006, Chad's then-president limited how much of oil-based income would be spent on development.

Chad was a destination for Sudanese refugees escaping the conflict in Darfur in 2004. In 2008, the European Union (EU) sent a peacekeeping force to protect refugees fleeing from violence in Darfur, Sudan, but ongoing violence continues between Chad and Sudan. By 2009, the violence was such that even international aid groups suspended their work due to excessive risk to their staff.

Justice for Chad's Ex-Dictator

Among the most notable human rights violations in central Africa were those that occurred under the regime of Hissene Habré, who was the dictator of Chad from 1982 to 1990. Survivors testified in a special court about violations including rape, torture, executions, and many other atrocities. In May 2016, Habré was finally found guilty of rape, torture, crimes against humanity, murder, mass summary execution, kidnapping and disappearing, inhuman treatment, forced slavery, and cruel treatment. He was sentenced to life imprisonment, and all his property was confiscated.

The trial was significant because it was the first time that the courts of one country (Senegal) prosecuted a former dictator of another country (Chad). This was accomplished through a special court, called the Extraordinary African Chambers, which the African Union created. It had taken twenty-five years of mobilization and requests by Hissene Habré's victims, aided by Human Rights Watch, Amnesty International, the United Nations, and other organizations, to get the case to trial. At the trial, more than four thousand victims were represented and 96 victims testified. It is estimated that 40,000 people had died under Habré's regime, and 1,208 died or were killed in detention. Other detainees suffered torture, rape, and sexual slavery, and there were 12,321 documented victims of human rights violations. Chad was left with 80,000 orphans. Ethnic groups attacked were the Hadjerai (in 1987) and the Zaghawas (in 1989).

According to the lead lawyer for the victims, Jacqueline Moudeina, the trial sent a message to all of Africa that "we dare to pursue and arrest those who do evil, who violate our rights. This is the great lesson we give to Chad and all of Africa ... it's the ability to fight against impunity."

The conviction was significant also because it was the first time that an international court held a former dictator responsible for rape. Said Reed Brody from Human Rights Watch, "Habré's conviction signals that no leader is above the law, and that no woman or girl is below it." Afterward, some of the women who testified reported that they finally felt empowered because they were able to speak their stories aloud while Habré listened silently.

Environmental Factors and Human Rights

Because of severe deforestation, the Batwa people (sometimes called Pygmies, although this is considered a derogatory term) have lost their forest home and traditional way of life. This has forced the Batwa to settle in villages or in camps for displaced persons, which in turn has led to violent conflicts between the Batwa and the Luba, an agricultural people.

Compounding the problem of survival, Lake Chad, which borders Chad, Niger, and CAR, has shrunk dramatically over the past fifty years (satellite images from

Blessed/Cursed with Riches

DR Congo is rich in copper, cobalt, timber, wildlife, water, oil, gold, zinc, and diamonds. Unfortunately for its people, this treasure has often brought exploitation. Joseph Conrad's 1899 book *Heart of Darkness* describes the exploitation Congolese people suffered under European colonialism in his narrative of a journey up the Congo River in the Congo Free State (as the region was then called).

After independence from Belgium, Congo has continued to be exploited by the wealthy elite of its government and by military groups that profit from war and unrest. The recent African world war, fought on Congolese soil, created opportunity for widespread looting and illicit financial flows—that is, money flowing out of the country to benefit a few wealthy individuals while the majority of the population is extremely poor.

The United Nations Economic Commission for Africa estimated that "between $1.2 trillion and $1.4 trillion left Africa in illicit financial flows between 1980 and 2009." This is money that should have benefited Africans but instead has been transferred elsewhere in the world. Meanwhile, it is believed that the money was generated from corruption, tax evasion, bribes, cross-border smuggling, and criminal activities.

NASA show a 95 percent decrease). This situation has caused a markedly smaller water supply for the nearby people. It also is an indicator of the kind of problems the world will have more of in the future as certain regions of the world dry out due to global climate change. Without water, people, along with their animals and crops, cannot survive.

What Is the Difference Between Congo and Democratic Republic of Congo?

The name "Congo" originates from the ancient kingdom of Kongo, which partly corresponds, though not exactly, to today's nations of DR Congo and Congo. (Kongo Kingdom included the Atlantic Coast, parts of today's DR Congo, and northern Angola). During colonization, the Kongo Empire was conquered, along with most of the continent, and the lands were divided and distributed among European nations and individuals. Belgian Congo (now Democratic Republic of Congo, or DR Congo) became the personal property of Belgian king Leopold, who exploited its natural and human resources for his personal gain to such an alarming extent that the Belgian people were troubled and took over administration of Congo as a state. Eventually DR Congo gained independence but has been governed by the same president since 2001, when Joseph Kabila took over following the death of his father (the previous President Kabila). As its name implies, DR Congo is theoretically a democracy, but elections do not always occur when scheduled. Today, DR Congo is the largest country in Africa, with its capital in Kinshasa. It still is very rich in resources—including gold, diamonds, timber, and other riches—even after centuries of exploitation. It has four national languages (Kikongo,

Lingala, Tshiluba, and Swahili) and far more dialects or tribal languages. President Joseph Kabila recently changed the number of provinces from eleven to twenty-six for unclear reasons. DR Congo is also home to Virunga National Park with white rhinoceroses, okapi, rare mountain gorillas, and bonobos, which are protected and found in no other country. This has created a sustainable tourism industry for the country, but tourism and the national park are both at risk—the forest is being burned for the charcoal industry.

The Republic of Congo, on the other hand, is a smaller country to the west of DR Congo. Its president is Denis Sassou N'Guesso, and its capital is Brazzaville. Both Congo and DR Congo have had their share of horrific wars in recent years, although DR Congo has seen more violence. Sassou N'Guesso came to power in 1979 and has remained there except for a brief period from 1992 to 1997. In 2016, he was named the winner in elections, having altered the constitution in order to be eligible for another term. He is criticized for repressing communications, the press, and other media. He has also been accused of corruption.

Africa's First World War

In DR Congo, from 1998 to 2003, a conflict raged that took the lives of more than five million people. It was called Africa's world war because many neighboring countries became involved, including Uganda, Rwanda, Zimbabwe, Namibia, and Angola. Although that conflict officially ended in 2003, a proxy war between Rwanda and the Kinshasa government (in DR Congo) continued until 2008. Various rebel groups still operate in eastern areas even now, destabilizing those areas. These rebel military groups (RMGs) recruit children and commit atrocities, including mass rapes and killings.

Unfortunately, these conflicts are typically funded by secret trading in the rich minerals and other natural resources found in central Africa. For example, the United States Justice Department claims that the Lord's Resistance Army (LRA) smuggled elephant ivory from Garamba National Park through the Central African Republic (CAR), South Sudan, and Sudan to finance its operations. Other resources that fund weapons include gold, tin ore, coltan, and rare earth metals used in cell phones, computers, and other devices. Another name for these activities is "illicit financial flows" because money and resources that should be benefitting the Congolese people are secretly flowing out of the country. This is a violation of the African Charter, which proclaims "the peoples' rights to development, free disposal of natural resources, and self-determination."

In the Democratic Republic of the Congo, commissions have investigated war crimes, crimes against humanity, murder, and sexual violence committed during the war. A 2010 UN report looked into the killings of Hutus saying they may constitute "crimes of genocide." The report also implicates Rwanda, Uganda, Burundi, Zimbabwe, and Angola. UN agencies reported on widespread rapes during mass expulsion of illegal migrants from Angola to DR Congo. Rape continues as a weapon of war even today, and victims suffer from physical and psychological injuries. Doctor Denis Mukwege and his staff at the Panzi clinic in Bukavu have been recognized for treating more than thirty thousand women who were victims. When he was threatened as a target, the women in his clinic showed their support and appreciation by deciding they would guard his life in groups of twenty—unarmed—so that he could continue his medical work to help them heal.

Although these human rights problems and ongoing clashes are real, significant, and ongoing, many ordinary Congolese (especially in urban centers like Kinshasa) enjoy normal lives. They pursue education, careers, and family life. They are proud of their country for its beauty, its wildlife, its diversity of cultures, and its many languages.

Gabon

About thirty ritual killings take place each year in Gabon, in which body parts are taken in order to bring special strength and power, according to traditional beliefs. Often the victims are young children, and their bodies wash up on the beach. Usually the requests for the killings are made by politicians, who pay poorer people to provide the organs. Little has been done by the Gabon government to put an end to this. While the killers are sometimes caught, the elected officials in power are not investigated. Ritual killings are not unique to Gabon, but they seem to be on the rise in that country. Most distressing is the apparent impunity with regard to these human sacrifices.

São Tomé and Príncipe: A Bastion of Human Rights

This small country fared the best in central Africa in terms of human rights. The only human rights issues reported were difficult prison conditions (though not nearly as severe as other central African countries, and not life-threatening), official corruption, domestic violence, and societal discrimination against women. In 2015, there were no reported extrajudicial killings or disappearances, no torture, and no political prisoners, and there was an increased number of consistently trained police officers, although citizens viewed them as ineffective and corrupt. The government is thought to generally respect freedoms of speech and the press, freedom of peaceful assembly and association, freedom of religion, and freedom to participate in elections.

Central African Human Rights in Context

Because of central Africa's incredibly rich resources, the global world cannot resist engaging in trade with these nations, even when the profits may be going to fund civil war, war crimes, and activities connected with genocide, torture, and terrorism. The film *Blood Diamond* revealed to Westerners how the romantic engagement ring and its industry were unfortunately connected to the African world war. Awareness prompted efforts to provide certification for diamonds, tracking their origins and ensuring that the diamonds purchased by Americans would not have cost the lives or limbs of innocents in DR Congo. Similar problems still exist, however, with other resources such as the rare earth minerals used in cell phones and other digital devices. More work needs to be done to ensure that those who benefit from global trade are not doing so at the expense of human rights in central Africa.

The current global refugee crisis, which is the worst in recorded history, includes people groups from both central African countries and those residing as displaced people within these countries. Support is needed from the international community to create stability so that people will again be free and safe in their own lands. In 2016, Federica Mogherini, high representative of the European Union (EU), urged the EU and the rest of the international community to work together with the UN to bring peace, freedom, and stability to Burundi, CAR, and DR Congo in particular.

Drought requires that this mother and her small children walk a long distance across barren landscape seeking water.

4 | Eastern Africa

The African Union designates the following countries as part of eastern Africa: Comoros, Djibouti, Eritrea, Ethiopia, Kenya, Madagascar, Mauritius, Rwanda, Seychelles, Somalia, South Sudan, Sudan, and the United Republic of Tanzania. Included in this region is "the Horn of Africa," composed of Djibouti, Eritrea, Ethiopia, and Somalia, which together appear on a map in the shape of a horn. Comoros, Madagascar, Mauritius, and Seychelles are islands in the Indian Ocean.

Historically, some of these countries have had complex relationships with one another; Ethiopia has ruled over Somalia; Eritrea was formerly part of Sudan; Sudan and South Sudan were once joined and formerly part of Egypt. In recent years, Kenya and Tanzania have been relatively stable countries surrounded by unstable neighbors. Areas with significant conflict tend to have fewer human rights protections, so eastern Africa faces significant challenges. Drought and famine exacerbate conflicts as different tribes compete for limited water and grazing land. Because there are thirteen countries in eastern Africa, and some of them experience more severe human rights issues than others, this chapter will focus on the most significant.

It is important to recognize that much of Africa is peaceful and nearly all regions have improved significantly in education, health, and poverty reduction over the past few decades. In fact, positive strides in human rights have been made in some parts of eastern Africa, such as in Tanzania, which recently elected a woman as vice president, putting it ahead of some of the more developed Western nations in terms of opportunities for women to participate in the highest levels of government. Other improvements include a rising rate of education and employment, a stable government, and freedoms of expression and association.

On the other hand, human rights in Kenya are deteriorating. Groups like Al-Shabaab create instability in the neighboring regions and have led to massive inflows of refugees from Kenya's neighbors into its refugee camps. In the face of encroaching terrorist groups, the government's response has been to restrict human rights in favor of security (although human rights experts would argue that history has shown that terrorism becomes weaker as citizens gain more rights).

Some countries in eastern Africa are extremely repressive—Eritrea, for instance, has been criticized by Amnesty International and other organizations for its violations of human rights. The United Nations 2015 report went as far as to accuse the Eritrean government of crimes against humanity and recommended that it be referred to the International Criminal Court (ICC). Some have compared its repressive regime to that of North Korea, although the Eritrean government denies similarities. Eritrea's president, Isaias Afwerki, has been in power since 1991—longer than Eritrea has been an independent country—becoming more repressive as time goes on.

Under this regime, Eritrean men younger than fifty years old are forced to serve in the military, often for longer terms than stated by law, where they are not provided adequate food. The Eritrean government considers men who emigrate to be traitors and deserters. The UN's human rights commission chair Mike Smith said, "The crimes of enslavement, imprisonment, enforced disappearance, torture, persecution, rape, murder and other inhumane acts have been committed as part of a widespread, systematic campaign against the civilian population since 1991." This explains why in 2015, more than forty-seven thousand Eritreans applied for asylum in Europe. Eritrea has been a country for just twenty-five years, and it continues to clash with Ethiopia, from which it declared independence.

Restrictions in Ethiopia

Among the biggest rights concerns in Ethiopia is government repression of freedoms. Citizens and aid workers are not allowed to criticize the government in any way; even reporting on the current hunger crisis is risky. The Ethiopian government has denied the presence of famine in spite of satellite imagery that depicts the drought.

In Ethiopia, human rights organizations and NGOs are not allowed to engage in "peace work," nor address rights issues and harmful traditional practices, engage in conflict transformation or peacebuilding, or do any advocacy. Such work would imply that problems exist in Ethiopia, which the government denies.

NGOs are able to work in some areas, including addressing revenge killings, women's and children's health, gender-based violence, intertribal conflict, and land rights. Conservation activities are also allowed in order to improve food security in Ethiopia.

Intertribal and International Conflict

Sudan, South Sudan, Eritrea, Ethiopia, and Somalia are considered the least stable parts of the continent. Somalia has not yet had a functional government in many decades. Unstable regions tend to be breeding grounds for human rights violations—both from various armed groups and from the governments that attempt to crack down on them. In such regions, civilian rights are not well protected. One Sudanese student in the United States, when asked about human rights in his country, said, "You Westerners care about human rights. In my country, we do not have rights. We are glad to not starve." Although human rights are inborn to every person regardless of his or her nation's legal system, it is true that South Sudanese do not have official protections, as South Sudan is the only country in Africa that has not ratified the African Charter on Human and Peoples' Rights (as of 2016).

South Sudan, Africa's youngest country, became independent from Sudan in 2011 following a bloody civil war. South Sudan is still not at peace, as rival tribes continue to torment one another. In fact, it is at present in full-on civil war.

The problems of instability in the Horn of Africa are exacerbated by severe droughts and famine, leading to conflicts over basic needs for survival. As people struggle to leave their countries in search of better livelihoods, conflicts spill into the neighboring countries.

Water! Water Is a Human Right …

During the past twelve years, the horn of Africa has gotten drier, even to the point of famine. In 2011 the area saw the greatest drought in more than sixty years, which caused food insecurity in Ethiopia, Eritrea, Djibouti, Kenya, and Somalia. Climate scientists anticipate further drying in the Horn of Africa as temperatures rise from carbon emissions worldwide. The United Nations addressed this very issue when it passed a resolution in 2010 recognizing water and sanitation as basic human rights.

Journalist Eliza Grizwold, in her book *The Tenth Parallel: Dispatches from the Fault Line Between Christianity and Islam*, discusses how lack of access to water and grazing lands leads to violent conflict. Religion is often blamed for regional conflicts, but often the real battle is over scarce resources, with religion or kinship as mere categories of identity around which people organize into groups as they compete for water and food. In times of drought and famine, conflicts escalate; where resources are plentiful, conflicts tend to diminish.

A common pattern of conflict in eastern Africa occurs between people groups who traditionally live as pastoralists, or seminomadic, and those who participate in agriculture. Tribes that historically follow the water and the seasons find themselves at odds, often violently, with those who have permanently settled in a specific region. In Kenya, the Samburu people are a pastoralist people who are discriminated against and sometimes killed in cattle-grazing conflicts.

Governments attempt to provide access to water for their people in various ways. Kenya plans to construct a mega-dam called Crocodile Jaws, intended to help the country develop and provide consistent access to water. The drawback of constructing this dam, however, is that it would flood the lands on which certain indigenous peoples' rights and livelihoods depend, including the Samburu and others.

Conservation Refugees

Conservation is generally considered a good thing because it means that governments and nongovernmental environmental groups wish to preserve natural resources, protect endangered animals, and create parks that generate income from tourists who come to enjoy them. The downside is that sometimes, in the process of setting aside these lands, certain people groups—those who wish to maintain a traditional way of life—have been forcibly removed from land where they have hunted and gathered, or grazed their cattle, for centuries. Such people are called indigenous because, although most Africans are native to their continent, these minority groups choose to maintain their ancient ways rather than to embrace external notions of development. The Samburu people in Kenya are one example of an indigenous people group whose rights are threatened.

According to the UN special report on the Status of Rights of the Samburu Indigenous Child (2015), around 85 percent of Samburu families live on less than $1.25 a week, which means that nearly the entire population meets the World Bank's definition of people living in extreme poverty. Housing, medical care, and basic nutrition remain huge obstacles for the Samburu. As a result, they are vulnerable to illness, starvation, and lack of access to education.

Strategies for Preventing Genocide

As troubling as genocide is, the phenomenon has occurred often enough throughout history that well-informed people can recognize the patterns that lead up to it and take strategic action to prevent it. Remembering the Rwanda genocide, the United Nations secretary-general Ban Ki-Moon said in 2014, "Twenty years ago, we saw, yet again after the Holocaust, how genocide is not a single event, but it is a process that evolves over time, a process that requires planning and resources. This also means that genocide can be prevented—with information and mobilization, as well as with courage and political will."

Ban Ki-Moon explained how the UN has since created an early warning system to sound the alarm "where there is a risk of genocide and other atrocities." Furthermore, he said, countries can help to prevent genocide by building "inclusive

Colonial Roots of Today's Conflicts

Eastern Africa is called the Cradle of Humanity because the earliest known human bones were discovered in this region. Eastern and central Africa are also perhaps the most diverse in terms of languages, tribes, and ethnic identities. This richness has a dark side, as some of these diverse tribes take negative views of one another, leading to extreme violence that goes well beyond a natural competition for resources.

During the 1990s, the global community was shocked to learn of a civil war in Rwanda playing out between two different ethnic groups, Hutus and Tutsis, each attempting to wipe out the other. The death toll amounted to nearly one million Rwandans killed after just one hundred days in 1994. The majority of those killed were Tutsis. The seed of this conflict was planted in colonialism, when British administrators favored the Tutsi people (a minority group) over the Hutus (the majority). After independence, the Hutus gained the upper hand in government and sought revenge on the people whom they associated with unjust colonial rule.

Left to Tell, by Immaculée Ilibagiza, tells the author's story of hiding for ninety-one days in her pastor's cramped bathroom with seven other women in order to escape the genocide. Journalist Jean Hatzfled reported on the Rwandan genocide in his book *Machete Season: The Killers in Rwanda Speak*. Hatzfled's book aims to place the unspeakable violence of the Rwandan genocide into context.

institutions and tolerant societies focusing on the resolution of grievances and of disputes through peaceful means." He cited several countries that have established national institutions for the prevention of genocide: Kenya, Rwanda, South Sudan, Tanzania and Uganda. He advises that,

> All societies should assess their vulnerability and work at every level to build **resilience**, to build tolerance and to build vigilance in detecting early warning signals … It means ensuring that the rule of law is respected and that all human rights are protected without discrimination. It means managing diversity, supporting a strong civil society and allowing all peoples' voices to be heard … We must do more as a community of nations and as global citizens if we are to live up to the promise of "never again" and act upon our collective responsibility to protect.

Today, as ethnic conflicts smolder throughout much of eastern Africa, especially in South Sudan, in the Darfur region of Sudan, and in Uganda, there is dire need to follow Ban Ki-Moon's advice and reduce the chances of genocide. While not all stakeholders agree on the best specific course of action, it is clear that without dramatic changes, more lives will be ruined—and some groups are at risk of extinction.

Gender Issues

Many times, traditional roles and gender-related practices are at odds with contemporary ideas of development and human rights. Some subcultures do not expect women to be educated because they have traditionally been thought of as the property of the community or of their fathers and husbands; therefore, they have no need of education or the ability to sustain a livelihood. Women have traditionally been excluded from participation in governance.

Somalia also has the highest rate of FGM/C of any country and the most extreme form. About 98 percent of women have experienced this. FGM/C is also practiced in many other countries but is more concentrated in eastern African countries.

Kenya and Its Neighbors: The Global Refugee Crisis

Migration and refugee issues pose great challenges, and Kenya is no exception. Refugees from South Sudan, Somalia, and Eritrea have fled to Kenya and Ethiopia. Somali Kenyans and other Muslim Kenyans face discrimination in the wake of terrorist attacks perpetrated by Al-Shabaab. Kenya is slowly getting more oppressive, curtailing media rights. Antiterrorist laws in both Kenya and Ethiopia are being misused to quash opposition and the media.

In a more positive direction, however, according to the UN, Kenya "passed a mining bill that is compliant with human rights standards and benefited from public consultations with key stakeholders during the drafting process, including the Kenya National Commission on Human Rights and civil society organizations." This shows that Kenya has not lost sight of the need to consider human rights in its laws.

In May of 2016, however, Kenya announced its intention to close down two refugee camps, including one in Dadaab (located in Garissa), which is the world's largest, and another in Kakuma (in Turkana). Kenya's principal secretary for

One Woman's Initiative to Save Mothers and Babies

Edna Adan Ismail, former first lady and foreign minister of Somalia, was born in Hargeisa, in what is now Somaliland, the daughter of a Somali medical doctor. She trained as a nurse and in 1980 began to work on building a new hospital in

Edna Adan Ismail

Somalia. Because of civil war, however, she had to abandon the project and flee the country for a time. After working as a nursing advisor for the World Health Organization, she finally built her hospital, the Edna Adan Maternity Hospital, in 2002. The facility is dedicated to training nurses and midwives in order to improve maternal health and infant survival, and to halt the practice of FGC/M, which is the primary reason why Somalia has such a high rate of complications and death related to childbirth. Somaliland has the worst maternal mortality rate in the world, with seventy-three deaths out of one thousand births. About 90 percent of these deaths are preventable, but less than 10 percent of births are assisted by skilled personnel. One in ten Somalian children does not survive the first year, but at the Edna Adan Hospital, the rates are much better. In the words of Edna Adan Ismail, "Don't ever underestimate the capacity of a human being who is determined to do something."

the Interior explained this was because the country "was no longer able to continue to shoulder the heavy economic, security, and environmental burden of hosting over 600,000 refugees for almost a quarter of the century."

The Kenyan government perceives these refugee camps as increasing the chances of terrorist attacks by groups like Al-Shabaab. Since Kenya's armed forces invaded Somalia in 2011 in pursuit of the terrorist organization Al-Shabaab, Kenya has endured more than one hundred terror attacks. Al-Shabaab's deadliest attack was in 2015 when the militants stormed Garissa University and massacred 148 students. The government has also disbanded the Department of Refugee Affairs.

Acknowledging the negative effects the camp closures will have on the lives of refugees, the government of Kenya has requested support from the international community in order to minimize pain and suffering. As of September 2015, the two camps together housed about 400,000 people; Dadaab alone has about 340,000 refugees while Kakuma has more than 55,000, according to UNHCR data.

Dadaab, which is 50 miles (80 km) from Somalia's border, was set up by the UN in 1991 for Somalis fleeing violence and famine in their home country. Kenya plans to repatriate all Somali refugees; as of mid-2016, 4,214 Somali refugees had been returned to Somalia under the UNHCR-assisted program. Some have criticized returning the refugees to their homeland given the violence and instability that likely awaits them upon return.

Somalia

Somalia is notorious among its neighbors for long-term instability. This instability leads to a lack of basic human rights protection for its people. Abuses have been committed from various fronts, including the former Somali government under Siad Barre, the Ethiopian military, which invaded Somalia, Al-Shabaab, and many other armed groups. According to the Office of the High Commissioner for Human Rights:

> Somalia has suffered a human rights crisis for the last 20 years, characterized by serious violations of human rights and humanitarian law. The protection of civilians in the context of the armed conflict, combined with impunity and lack of accountability, is of major concern. The lack of rule of law and the climate of insecurity has created an environment in which certain categories of professionals, such as journalists and judges, are increasingly targeted for extrajudicial killings. An entire generation has grown up without access to education and the country as a whole suffers from a lack of knowledge about human rights. Women and children's rights are routinely violated.
>
> The collapse of the humanitarian situation has further aggravated the human rights crisis and resulted in massive displacement of Somalis from the Southern regions into TFG-controlled territories and across the borders into Ethiopia and Kenya. The vulnerability of the displaced has raised acute protection concerns. In the margins of the 18th session of the Human Rights Council, the Office of the High Commissioner for Human Rights has advocated for a human rights based approach to the

Somalia, on the whole, is considered a failed state. When one Nigerian student staying in the United States was asked what should be included in a book about human rights in Africa, he responded, "Not Somalia!" Similarly, a Kenyan woman said, "We don't understand Somalia. It is always unstable."

Globally, Somalia is infamous for its pirates, people smugglers, and malnourished children. Yet Somalia has seen better times, such as during the 1970s, when hospitals, schools, and government functioned. Some blame tribalism, some blame the former Barre regime, and others blame ill-planned interventions from outsiders that have failed to include the traditional elder-based justice system that formed the core of Somali societal structure for time immemorial— well before colonialism, nationalism, and modernization.

Somalia, Somaliland, and Puntland

Although the situation in Somalia is dire, it is worth noting that portions of the country are relatively peaceful. Somaliland is a self-declared independent state in the north that has experienced relative peace for the past two decades while the remainder of the country has been a failed state. Something different happened in Somaliland because of grassroots efforts to make peace from the ground up rather than a top-down effort. In 1991, as the central government of Somalia collapsed, the northern region of Somalia declared itself independent and called itself Somaliland. Puntland is an adjacent region, which has also experienced relative peace. This is because of the efforts of traditional elders and leaders, women's groups, and local people who created a series of

A tree where people gather for traditional meetings in Belet Weyne, central Somalia, north of Mogadishu

meetings with one another to reconcile different clans and subclans, ending fighting and addressing their grievances with one another. A grand reconciliation conference was held in Borama in 1994. While international nongovernmental organizations provided funding and logistics, the local people implemented the actual peacemaking process, drawing on their traditional structures and knowledge to resolve conflicts.

Eighty-two elders, representing all the clans in Somaliland, provide stable governance.

In contrast, the rest of Somalia has been subjected to numerous interventions by outside forces, backed variously by the United Nations, the African Union, the Ethiopian government, and the United States, which have systematically failed to understand or include the traditional roles and leadership of clan elders. These elders had been responsible for peacemaking prior to the Barre regime. The top-down, outsider-run approach, where decisions have been made at meetings outside the country of Somalia and imposed on the local people, has failed to create lasting peace and stability.

The current president of Somalia, Hassan Sheikh Mohamud, however, is highly educated in international peace studies and has initiated new efforts designed to offer full participation to all clans and parties. Under his leadership, camps have been set up to provide a way out for former Al-Shabaab fighters who wish to leave the organization and begin a normal life.

Special Human Rights Issue: People with Albinism

It is estimated that one in 5,000 to 15,000 people in sub-Saharan Africa have a genetic condition called albinism, which affects melanin pigments in skin, hair, and eyes. World Health Organization statistics say that "albinism affects about one in 17,000 to 20,000 people in Europe and North America," but in parts of Africa, the rate of occurrence is much higher. In Tanzania, about one in 1,400 people are thought to carry the gene (offspring need to receive the gene from both parents in order for it to be expressed). About 170,000 people with albinism live in Tanzania, although the population is difficult to track because many individuals affected by albinism live in hiding.

Because of superstitious beliefs, these people are often targeted for killing or for amputation of their body parts, which are made into potions thought to produce wealth (*muti*); other people believe that a person with albinism is a ghost or may bring bad luck if he or she is allowed to live in the community. From 2000 to 2014, at least 73 persons with albinism were killed in Tanzania for ritual purposes.

In addition, albinism can be deadly for natural reasons; the lack of pigment can cause low vision, and constant sunburn results in high rates of cancer. Lack of access to medical care, to sunscreen, and to other simple preventive measures means that most people with albinism in sub-Saharan Africa die before age forty. In Tanzania, 90 percent of people with albinism do not live to age thirty.

To help cope, the Tanzanian government has set up centers where persons with albinism can live in safety, called temporary holding centers (THC). Many of the children and adults who live there have previously been attacked, sometimes by members of their own families, so the centers are located in compounds with concrete walls and are locked after nightfall. Sadly, the centers are overcrowded and often lack the necessary resources to provide quality care for the children who live there. Organizations such as the Red Cross, Under the Same Sun (founded on behalf of people with albinism), UNICEF, and faith-based groups provide aid.

Eastern African Human Rights in Context

More than ever before, the situation in eastern African countries affects the rest of the world because this is the primary source of the greatest refugee crisis seen in modern times. Refugees from Sudan, South Sudan, Ethiopia, Eritrea, and Somalia are flooding into Europe across the Mediterranean Sea, literally risking their lives for a chance to live in a country where their human rights and dignity will be respected.

Terrorist groups based in eastern Africa, including Al-Shabaab, al-Qaeda, and others now threaten the security of European nations, Britain, and the United States. Isolationism is not possible in our globally connected world. Seen positively, refugees are a rich resource to the nations that accept them, bringing their hosts rich diversity, broader understanding, greater empathy, and deeper awareness of the human condition.

Nelson Mandela has inspired worldwide movements to reduce discrimination based on race.

5 Southern Africa

C ountries that make up southern Africa include Angola, Botswana, Lesotho, Malawi, Mozambique, Namibia, South Africa, Swaziland, Zambia, and Zimbabwe. All of these are located on the mainland. Overall, southern Africa is presently more stable than western, central, and eastern Africa, but southern African countries bear their share of human rights issues nonetheless. Some of the most significant issues have to do with the use and distribution of natural resources, whereby governments choose to utilize resources in ways that do not necessarily benefit the local people. This is especially a problem in places where water is exported, as in Lesotho, leaving shortages for the residents. It is also a problem in Angola, where a wealthy elite lives extremely comfortably while most people live on $2 per day or less.

Of southern African countries, human rights observers point to Zimbabwe and Angola as having the most severe abuses, and to South Africa as having made the greatest progress. Both good leadership and grassroots movements for positive change played significant roles in South Africa, while in Zimbabwe and Angola, government corruption delays progress in the areas of human rights, development, education, and democracy.

According to the UN, some southern African countries are categorized as "least developed countries" (LDC) while others have graduated from this designation. LDC are those that meet three criteria: "poverty (a gross national income of less than US $1,035 per person), human resource weakness (based on levels of nutrition, health, education, and literacy), and economic vulnerability (based on unstable agricultural production, instable exports of goods and services, displacement by natural disasters, and other factors)." Botswana (of southern Africa) and Cabo Verde (of western Africa) were no longer considered to be LDC by 2011. Angola, along with Equatorial Guinea, is expected to graduate soon. São Tomé and Príncipe met the criteria in March 2015. Many African nations are on the list of least developed countries.

Rising from poverty is often associated with a rise in respect for human rights. Therefore, as southern Africa develops sustainably and economically, the future of human rights will likely improve as well.

South Africa: A Key Player in Human Rights History

The nation of South Africa is considered a model nation for how human rights can dramatically improve in a relatively short period of time. Just a few decades ago, South Africa was a nation of apartheid, meaning that blacks and whites were kept separate and treated unequally. Comedian Trevor Noah, who hosts *The Daily Show*, recalled his experience of growing up as the child of a black mother and a white father in South Africa in an interview on America's National Public Radio. He said it was not safe for him to be seen walking the public streets with his mother because his skin color was evidence that his parents had crossed the color line. His mother was even jailed a

Nelson Mandela

Nelson Mandela is perhaps the best internationally known African figure because of his nonviolent work to create a South Africa without apartheid. He was imprisoned for twenty-seven years, but he was released in 1990 and became president of South Africa in 1994. He is known for his peaceful movement to bring equality for all people—whether black, "colored," white, or Indian—in his country as well as inspiring civil rights movements worldwide. He also spoke out about HIV/AIDS and helped to raise awareness about this health and social crisis in Africa. His Robben Island prison number, 46664, was used as the name of a global campaign to raise awareness about HIV/AIDS.

After his retirement from public life in 2004, he continued to positively influence the world. In 2007, Mandela and Archbishop Desmond Tutu gathered together a group of world leaders called the Elders to share their wisdom and leadership with regard to global problems. July 18 is called Nelson Mandela International Day, so named by the United Nations General Assembly to remember the antiapartheid struggle and to encourage individuals to donate time to help others.

Mandela passed away in 2013 at the age of ninety-five. President Obama of the United States said, "We've lost one of the most influential, courageous, and profoundly good human beings that any of us will share time with on this Earth. He no longer belongs to us—he belongs to the ages."

few times for her crime of having relations with a white man. In contrast, his white father was not punished because whites had greater protections and status in those years.

Today, however, South Africa has arguably made the greatest progress in racial equality. The country has its own Human Rights Commission, which provides accountability and protection for the rights of all persons. The South African Human Rights Commission (SAHRC) has set priorities to improve equal access to rights for all its people, "regardless of color, religion, disability, age, or any other factor." These strategic areas include "access to justice and housing; protections for those with disability and older persons; just use of the environment, natural resources and rural development; human rights and law enforcement and prevention of torture; providing basic services and health care; protecting children's rights and basic education; and migration and equality."

While it would be incorrect to claim that there are no human rights problems in South Africa today (every country, whether in Africa or elsewhere, continues to struggle and must be held accountable), South Africa has made huge strides. The nation has clear laws to protect human rights (including its constitution and bill of rights) and enforces these laws. Having a national human rights commission and other organizations focused on protecting human rights has created a dialogue: problems can be identified, discussed, and resolved. While human rights violations still happen, they are not tolerated.

With South Africa's constitution of 1994, the SAHRC was set up to "support constitutional democracy." According to the government, this commission is "committed to promote respect for, observance of and protection of human rights for everyone without fear or favour." The constitution mandates that the SAHRC must "promote respect for human rights and a culture of human rights; ... promote the protection, development and attainment of human rights; and ... monitor and assess the observance of human rights in the Republic."

Truth and Reconciliation Commission of South Africa

After the end of apartheid, there was a deep need for reconciliation and healing between different groups that had either suffered and/or committed gross violations of human rights during apartheid. Violations had been committed on all sides—from the state, military, and police, but also by groups that took up arms to resist apartheid. So a court-like body focused on restorative justice gathered together in order to allow both victims and offenders to tell their stories about their experiences. Some victims gave statements in public hearings. On the other side, perpetrators of violence provided their testimonies and asked for amnesty and forgiveness from prosecution. The purposes of this Truth and Reconciliation Commission (TRC) were to investigate human rights abuses that had occurred from 1960 to 1994 and create a venue for **reparations** and rehabilitation in a way that honors human dignity. Some victims (or their families) received reparations and educational scholarships. Some—not all—offenders received amnesty.

Although the TRC and the South African government recognized that many gross violations of human rights had happened prior to 1960, this limited time frame made the task more manageable. The year 1960 was chosen because this was about the time when liberation movements, such as the African National Congress (ANC) and the Pan Africanist Congress (PAC) and others, turned violent. While apartheid

Marching to End Pass Laws

In August of 1956, twenty thousand women of all races marched together in South Africa to protest a law that would require all African (black) women to carry passes. The law to carry passes was part of the system of apartheid that was enforced from 1948 to 1994. Starting in 1950, Parliament passed legislation dividing people into four categories of "race": white, black, "coloured" (mixed race), and Indian. Non-white South Africans were restricted in their rights to travel, to choose certain occupations, and in many other ways. The Group Areas Act designated specific areas of land for each racial group to live and work. Authorities could (and did) forcibly remove people from one place to another if they did not meet the correct racial profile. Many families were forcibly relocated according to race.

Upon hearing that nonwhite women would be forced to carry passes to travel into town, thousands of women mobilized in a way that Africa had never seen. Several different groups came together for anti-passbook campaigns, including the African National Congress Women's League and the nonracial Federation of South African Women, as well as various other groups. In their 1956 protest march, the women sang a song that includes a phrase that means, when translated, "You Strike a Woman, You Strike a Rock."

Here women protest violence against women in Lesotho on National Women's Day in 1994 to commemorate the 1956 Women's March.

itself was ruled a crime against humanity, some of the means used to resist it were also violations of human rights (such as killings and torture).

Although the TRC had its flaws and was criticized from all sides, the process took care to respond appropriately to all stakeholders: perpetrators, victims, and ordinary citizens who had committed no violations but regretted the legacy of the past and wished to build a better future for all parties. The African National Congress, the National Party, the military, and other groups testified about what they had done. Special hearings were also set up for various groups such as businesses, faith communities, the health sector, and even the Mandela United Football Club, to share how they had failed to respect human dignity.

In the five-volume final report of the TRC, Archbishop Desmond Tutu wrote the memorable words:

Having looked the beast of the past in the eye, having asked and received forgiveness and having made amends, let us shut the door on the past—not in order to forget it but in order not to allow it to imprison us. Let us move into the glorious future of a new kind of society where people count, not because of biological irrelevancies or other extraneous attributes, but because they are persons of infinite worth ...

The South African TRC has inspired many similar efforts conducted internationally, and it is generally considered to have been a vital component for the transition to the new, free, and more democratic South Africa. Similar Truth and Reconciliation Commissions have since been held in many other countries, such as Rwanda, in order to help heal societies after significant conflicts, genocide, and other traumas on civil society.

The Hunter-Gatherers of Southern Africa

A group of people known variously as Basarwa, San, Bushmen, or Khoisan are thought to be the most ancient people alive today. Different tribes prefer different names according to which ones are considered derogatory in their region. Archaeological evidence suggests they have lived in southern Africa (including parts of present-day South Africa, Botswana, Namibia, Zambia, and Zimbabwe) for tens of thousands of years. More than twenty thousand of their rock paintings are preserved in five hundred different sites. Traditionally, they are hunter-gatherer people living in the Kalahari Desert, but in recent decades they have lost access to much of their ancestral lands and many are unable to survive

In Botswana, young San/Bushmen start a fire with a wooden drill as their people have done for thousands of years.

in the old ways. Their complex language includes various clicks and other sounds.

Botswana created the Great Kalahari Game Park in 1961, partly to provide land for this people group to use in their traditional ways. Yet in the 1990s, the Botswanan government changed course, pushing instead for the San/Basarwa people to assimilate with settled people. They were given cattle and small plots of land, but many have not adjusted well to the new arrangement. With the loss of their traditional lifestyle, many have turned to alcoholism and domestic abuse, and some have fallen ill with diseases including tuberculosis and HIV/AIDS. Their highly developed skills in hunting, gathering, and relating to their environment have not transferred to cattle-rearing, so the livestock has not fared well either.

The San/Basarwa have faced discrimination, torture, and harassment, being insulted as "Stone Age" people and worse. Other tribal groups in Botswana regard them as subhuman or inferior to those who have a modern life. This has caused tension between those who wish to honor the agreements previously made to allow the San to continue to live in the game park and those who agree with the government's later decision to force them off the land and require them to settle. The Botswana online newspaper Mmegi published an opinion piece by Segametsi Modikela Letlhakeng in which the author compared the current plight of the Basarwa to the plight of blacks in South Africa during apartheid: "Every one of us must exercise an independent and critical mind when addressing the issue of forced relocation of Basarwa. We should not allow government to indoctrinate us and turn us into conformists."

In 2013, during a legal battle between the Basarwa and the government of Botswana, the government refused to allow the Basarwa's British lawyer, Gordon Bennett, to enter the country after he won two cases. By 2015, the Basarwa were said to be starving because all hunting was banned in 2014; the government claimed that the game animals needed to be conserved.

The organization Just Conservation, which supports conservation that is done with justice in mind, points out that some of the most successful conservation efforts worldwide have been those that integrated indigenous people into the preserves, allowing them to continue their traditions and help to protect the land and animals.

Angola's Limited Freedom of Expression

The US State Department identified the three most important human rights abuses in Angola in 2015 as "cruel, excessive and degrading punishment, including reported cases of torture and beatings; limits on freedoms of assembly, association, speech and press; and official corruption and impunity."

According to Human Rights Watch, the government targets journalists and peaceful activists, using "harassment, intimidation, and pervasive surveillance by police and intelligence agents." Freedom of expression is restricted by censorship and **self-censorship** (meaning that the press chooses not to report on issues that could get them into trouble with their government). Journalists are sometimes arrested without being charged and are forced to delete videos and other materials from their records.

Maternal and child mortality rates are among the highest in the world, indicating that the government is providing inadequate funding for health care. Meanwhile, Angola's president, Jose Eduardo dos Santos, who has ruled since 1979, has grown rich from the nation's oil and diamond industries. In June 2016, he sacked the board of Angola's state-owned oil company Sonangol and gave his daughter Isabel dos Santos the job of heading it. *Forbes* magazine named her Africa's eighth-richest person, worth an estimated $3.2 billion (as of June 2016). According to the BBC's Mary Harper, Angola had the "world's fastest growing economy from 2000-10," but all that wealth is held by just a few elite families. The UN's 2015 Human Development Index ranked Angola 149 out of 188 countries, and life expectancy at birth is just 52 years.

Rafael Marques de Morais's book *Blood Diamonds: Corruption and Torture in Angola* alleges that both army and private security companies have violated human rights in atrocious ways in order to profit from diamond mining. Angola is one of seven countries in which diamonds have helped to fund conflicts in recent decades (Angola's twenty-seven-year civil war ended in 2002). The other six are Sierra Leone, Liberia, Congo, DR Congo, Côte d'Ivoire, and the Central African Republic.

The Worth of Water in Lesotho and Zimbabwe

In June 2016, National Public Radio's Robert Smith from *Planet Money* covered a story on what has happened in Lesotho over the past five decades. Lesotho is a small African country located like an island within the country of South Africa. The country has been selling its water as a commodity to supply Johannesburg for more than fifty years. When water was plentiful, Lesotho agreed to a long-term contract with South Africa to provide the larger country with water. But now, the river that sources Johannesburg's dams is drying up. A woman from Lesotho, Blessing Nkhase, spoke with Smith in an interview, reciting British Lord Byron's poetic lines, "In short, till taught by pain, men know not what water is worth."

In Zimbabwe, too, water is a significant human rights issue. Even in Zimbabwe's big cities, like Harare (the capital) and Bulawayo, many people do not have access to clean water. Some use unprotected wells, which expose them to diseases. Cholera alone killed more than four thousand people between 2008 and 2009 and sickened one hundred thousand, according to Human Rights Watch. Its sixty-page report detailed conditions in 2012 and 2013, noting how Zimbabweans have "little access to potable water and sanitation services, and often resort to drinking water from shallow, unprotected wells that are contaminated with sewage, and to defecating outdoors. The conditions violate their right to water, sanitation, and health." In other communities, Human Rights Watch reported, contact with sewage causes diarrhea and typhoid. It is feared there will be another cholera epidemic if the government continues to do nothing about the problem.

According to the World Health Organization, several African countries have it worse. The WHO's figures show that only half of Angolans have access to improved sources of drinking water, and half have access to proper sanitation. In Zambia, 78 percent have access to water and 46 percent have access to sanitation; 60 percent of people in Swaziland have clean water, and 50 percent have sanitation. Botswana is doing better—96 percent of its people have clean water, although just 47 percent have access to sanitation. In Mozambique, just 42 percent have clean drinking water and 31 percent have access to sanitation.

Malawi's Women

It is estimated that one in two females in Malawi marries before age eighteen, making it one of the top countries for early (child) marriages. The problems with early marriage are that the girls do not have the opportunity to complete their education, and they often suffer pregnancy complications from their bodies being too small to deliver babies. This creates a higher risk of Caesarean sections, other health problems, and even maternal death. Early marriage also increases the risk of domestic abuse. Yet there is high pressure from parents to find spouses for their children early because of finances. Malawi is one of the world's poorest countries (90 percent of the population lives on less than $2 per day), so daughters are considered an expense to get rid of quickly.

In 2015, Malawi finally passed a law forbidding civil marriages for anyone under age eighteen, but customary (traditional) law, which is governed by tribal chiefs, still allows marriages to young girls, even girls as young as eleven or twelve. One head chief, Theresa Kachindamoto, decided to take on this human rights issue by asking all of her fifty

Chief Inkosi Theresa Kachindamoto, a powerful chief in Malawi, has broken up over eight hundred marriages of children and teenagers in order to send them back to school to complete their education.

subchiefs to sign a law abolishing early marriages under customary law. She has even gone so far as to personally break up 850 marriages of teenagers, sending the children back to school to complete their education for a better future.

Malawi has the prestigious honor of having had the second female president in the history of Africa. Joyce Banda was vice president in 2012 when President Mutharika died at age seventy-eight. The BBC reported that Mutharika's wife, Callista Mutharika, said of Banda, "She will never be president, how can a mandasi [fritter] seller be president?" Patricia Kaliati, the information minister, also said that Banda had no right to take over as president, despite what the constitution said.

After rising to office, Banda sacked Kaliati and said that she was proud to be a mandasi seller, since more than 60 percent of women in Malawi are market women.

Corruption as an Obstacle to Human Rights

The organization Transparency International keeps detailed records and analyzes which countries throughout the world are more corrupt and which are more transparent. Experts grade each country on a scale of one to one hundred, with more points being awarded to countries that are transparent. According to its 2015 Corruption Perceptions Index, the most corrupt countries are Angola, South Sudan, Sudan, Afghanistan, North Korea, and Somalia. The least corrupt are Denmark, Finland, Sweden, New Zealand, the Netherlands, and Norway. The United States came in sixteenth place, with a score of seventy-six, up slightly from the previous two years' data.

Any country that scores below fifty is considered to have a serious corruption problem, and most southern African countries fall in that zone. Angola, already mentioned, scored only fifteen points. Lesotho received forty-four points, while Malawi and Mozambique each got thirty-one, South Africa got forty-four, Zambia got thirty-eight, and Zimbabwe got twenty-one, making it almost as corrupt as Angola. Namibia rose to fifty-three (after scoring below fifty points in previous years). Swaziland was not studied. Botswana did remarkably well, scoring sixty-three points and ranking twenty-third overall for its ethical status.

Clearly, corruption is an area for improvement for most of southern Africa—especially for Angola. Corruption affects human rights because if a government and the justice system can be paid off by bribery or favors, then justice is not likely to be served.

Two-thirds of the land in Swaziland is controlled by the king in this last remaining monarchy in Africa.

Swaziland: The Last Monarchy in Africa

The small nation of Swaziland is tucked into a corner of South Africa. According to the Swaziland government's website, it is a monarchy that follows the traditional line of kings that have led the people since the fifteenth and sixteenth centuries, when Africans of Nguni descent migrated from central Africa into what is today Swaziland. These people are today known as either Swazis or Nkosi Dlamini. Dlamini is the surname of the royal family, which dates back to about 1550. Swaziland was a protectorate of South Africa and then of the British from 1902 until independence in 1968. Due to the very specific pattern of kingship, the nation has been ruled by either its king or, when the king was too young, by the queen mother or regent. The king must choose wives from several different clans in order to ensure unity.

Amnesty International points out that Swaziland is the last monarchy in Africa. Although a new constitution came into being in 2006, human rights are narrow in its bill of rights, and the government restricts them even more. According to Amnesty International, women and girls are second-class citizens in this country, and no laws exist against early or forced marriage. Girls can be married as young as age thirteen under customary law—against their will. Two-thirds of the lands are controlled by the king and his chiefs, and families can be forcibly removed if they openly express dissent from the royal family. Freedoms of speech and expression are virtually nonexistent.

Southern African Human Rights in Context

This chapter highlighted only a few of the human rights issues facing southern African countries in the twenty-first century. Basic rights to water and survival are most vital to the impoverished nations. The greatest obstacle to achieving this is government corruption. Greater protections for women, such as the reduction of child marriages and more opportunities for participation in government, will benefit human rights for all southern Africans. Marginalized people, such as the San people, may have the most to lose when land rights are disputed.

But against this backdrop, southern Africa has made great success in some areas. South Africa has made a dramatic turnaround from its apartheid years to welcoming Nelson Mandela as president. Mandela inspired nations worldwide to do better work to improve race relations and peaceful transformations to society.

As more Africans migrate to cities for modern work and life, rural people like this Samburu family become rarer and more marginalized.

6 The Future of Human Rights Throughout Africa

What does the future hold for Africans and their human rights? This is a large question, and perhaps it is best answered by looking backward to see how far Africa has come. In a relatively short time, the continent of Africa has been transformed from a collection of colonies with little control over their own futures to a thriving community of fifty-four (more or less, depending on the disputed status of SADR and Somaliland) unique and independent countries—albeit, admittedly, with varying degrees of health and development.

As Dr. Martin Luther King Jr. once said, "Injustice anywhere is a threat to justice everywhere." These inspiring words remind us, decades after his death, that the rights of each human being is connected to the rights of every other person in our world. Injustice cannot be tolerated or ignored because it has a way of spreading to those around it.

In our increasingly connected global community, all global citizens have an unprecedented opportunity to participate in justice issues both close to home and abroad. With so many activists lending their best efforts to improve human rights wherever they find the opportunity, good changes are sure to happen. Culture is never static. It is always in flux. Every generation has the privilege and the responsibility—the right—to shape that culture for good or for ill.

It can be said that Africans and their supporters are situated at a tremendously hopeful time in history where so much has been accomplished: the legal abolition of slavery, the end of colonization, the start of independence for many nations, and the forming of institutions and mechanisms for justice. Consider the African Union, the **African Court**, the African human rights commissions, and the wealth of countless other organizations, both local grassroots and international, devoted to improving human rights for Africans and all peoples.

It is equally true that Africans and their supporters are situated at a daunting time in history where so much is yet to be done: ameliorating the devastating effects of climate change, investigating and trying human rights violators in credible courts of law, and providing opportunities for all people to participate fully in their society, whether male or female, young or old, majority or minority status, with or without disability, whether victim or offender (or both). Think of what will be needed for girls and women to reach their full potential, or for unemployed young men in need of a better option than becoming soldiers, or of people with disabilities or albinism or LGBTI individuals looking for acceptance.

Dire Straits

It is chilling to know that many marginalized groups are under threat of genocide and mass killings due to their ethnic, religious, health, or other status. An organization called Minority Rights Group International has developed a way to calculate which groups in particular are most at risk of being targeted. It has even created an index of Peoples Under Threat. Based on its calculations (as of June 2016), there are five African countries most at risk for genocide and mass killings: Somalia, Sudan, South Sudan, Democratic Republic of Congo, and Central African Republic. Other African countries worth noting are Libya, Algeria, and Burundi. After reading this book, perhaps it is not surprising to hear these countries named. But the Peoples Under Threat Index provides the following rationales, summarized below:

- Actions and advances by Al-Shabaab rebels into Kenya explain why Somalia remains in danger. The Bantu minority population is particularly at risk, as many of them fill the Dadaab refugee camp in Kenya that is scheduled to close.

- South Sudan and Sudan continue to clash in spite of their peace agreement; ethnic components contribute to the tension. Sudan's government frequently targets its own civilians.

- DR Congo hosts clashes between Bantu and Batwa, along with attacks from the Lord's Resistance Army and other militia groups. Drivers include ethnic factors, competition for resources, cross-border conflicts, and retaliation.

- Central African Republic continues to see conflicts between Muslim pastoralists and Christian farmers.

- Libya shows little sign of recovering from its failed state. Between the competing militias, rivaling tribes, and the expansion of ISIS, it is expected to get even worse before it will get better.

- Algeria struggles with both communal conflict between Arah and Mosabite (Amasigh) communities and external confrontations between Algerian military and various radical Islamist groups (al-Qaeda and others). Other ethnic divisions pose problems as well.

- The current crisis in Burundi is strikingly similar to the pattern seen in Rwanda's past, where attempted genocide tore the country apart for years. Targeted killings are already taking place in Burundi, causing 250,000 people to flee, and there is fear that things might return to the terrible times of the past.

Resilience and Empowerment

As terrible as some situations have been and will likely continue to be so for some time, better circumstances are inevitable, too. Wherever people suffer, there will also be resilience. Wherever strong battles rage, people will become empowered to fight them. Africa's history is illuminated with the stories of strong women and men who have stood up for rights and justice, who have been fearless in their pursuit of making their countries better, who have persisted in envisioning a better future and working toward that dream.

The African Union's Agenda 2063: The Africa We Want

Africans know what they want for the future. The African Union clearly articulated that in its agenda of what it plans to work toward in the future in a document called "Agenda 2063: The Africa We Want." The year 2063 was chosen because it was fifty years into the future from when these activists and visionaries met together to create this agenda in 2013. Not all of this agenda relates directly to human rights, but this collective body recognizes that human rights will be integral to any sustainable development for a bright future in Africa.

As with all great visions, there are sure to be fits and starts and occasional steps back in the midst of progress, but with continued perseverance and support from the international community, Agenda 2063 can be achieved. Some of the aspirations for 2063 published on the African Union's website relate directly to human rights issues:

ASPIRATION 3:

An Africa of good governance, democracy, respect for human rights, justice and the rule of law.

Africa shall have a universal culture of good governance, democratic values, gender equality, respect for human rights, justice and the rule of law …

ASPIRATION 6:

An Africa whose development is people-driven, relying on the potential of African people, especially its women and youth, and caring for children.

All the citizens of Africa will be actively involved in decision making in all aspects. Africa shall be an inclusive continent where no child, woman or man will be left behind or excluded, on the basis of gender, political affiliation, religion, ethnic affiliation, locality, age or other factors …

Empowerment and Development

On its website ECOWAS features a documentary film called *Think Again*, showcasing the prominent role that women can play in the burgeoning power industry in western African nations.

The film highlights the stories of a number of west African women who work in the energy sector, a male-dominated field. Reliable sources of electricity are needed in order to meet human needs for agriculture, health care, education, and more. By including women as leaders in these projects, women become more independent and empowered. With empowerment, women become less vulnerable to gender-based violence. In addition, they are better equipped to provide well for their children, which will strengthen the up-and-coming generation. These children will then have better nutrition, better education, and higher quality of life than the generation that came before them.

Ultimately, when women benefit, their families—including men and children—will benefit, too. Women will play a central role in Africa's future, as they will be active participants in the new economy and the new future. As women become empowered, they will in turn empower their communities— just as they are already doing in many places.

In order to achieve the goals of this agenda, many incremental steps will need to be taken. For example, careful and sustainable economic development will help alleviate the poverty that contributes to sources of conflict. In addition, reduced corruption and impunity, along with greater pressure to address and reduce human rights violations, will likely lead to positive changes in the lives of most Africans.

People will continue to work toward improving human rights, through legislation and through enforcement. Just as other nations such as Denmark, Finland, Sweden, New Zealand, the Netherlands, Norway, the United States, and many others have gradually and incrementally developed better human rights structures and protections, both at the legislative and the justice level, African nations will, too. The African Court handled its first case in 2009; justice is on the rise.

As more African countries become familiar with democratic processes, elections will undoubtedly become calmer affairs with less power grabbing by would-be dictators. Education and health care will continue to improve as both the international community and national governments invest in them.

Yet one of the great challenges Africa faces already, which is expected to worsen as the climate changes, is the impacts of increasing drought, floods, and erratic weather patterns. Weather-related crises will bring more conflict and instability to the Sahel region

Students working in their school's computer lab in Kyeizooba Bushenyi Secondary School, Uganda as Lake Chad continues to dry up and the Horn of Africa experiences increasing dryness. Without provisions for basic human needs like water and food, security will be elusive. Without security, human rights become more vulnerable to abuse. It remains to be seen whether the international community will have the ability or the political will to reduce the human portion of the impact on climate. Innovation in agriculture and irrigation will help to mitigate the problems, but all countries worldwide should prepare and plan now how to manage and adjust to new weather patterns and a new climate.

How Can Africa Continue to Bolster Human Rights?

The number one goal for improving the protections for human rights on the continent of Africa—and worldwide—is education. Sadly, many people continue to carry on their lives unaware that they have such a thing as "rights." As John C. Mugangizi wrote in an article in *Human Rights Law Journal,*

> The enjoyment of human rights largely depends on the level of awareness of what these rights are and how to enforce them. Human rights education (HRE), therefore, is crucial in ensuring that people are empowered to access the rights to which they are entitled.

Therefore, perhaps the most important action to be taken is to educate and raise awareness about the importance of human rights and the need to promote and protect these rights for all people. For Africa's future, human rights–based education will continue to be a powerful force to help people solve their own problems and make their own choices, giving them more options as to how to develop themselves and resolve conflicts. African nations will no longer be controlled by foreign powers. Instead, Africa will grow in freedom and independence—yet the continent will retain the interconnectedness, the communal values, and the understanding that human rights come with responsibilities and obligations to families, communities, countries, and neighbors. It will be vital to improve educational systems and access to education for all citizens, especially for females and the poor who are often unable to afford school fees and uniforms. Curriculum should include training in nonviolence, trauma resilience, and peace building.

Sustainable development, when accomplished with a human rights–based approach, will help to reduce poverty, which will in turn reduce risk of crime and lessen the chance that people will resort to violence. This includes ongoing improvements to infrastructure (that is, access to clean water and sanitation services, consistent electricity, roads, and other transportation systems) in order to provide improved quality of life as well as respectable business opportunities.

Reducing corruption in countries where that is a significant problem, as indicated on the Transparency Index, will be necessary in order for each nation's wealth to be used for the benefit of all its citizens. This will require action both within countries (from courageous individuals) and from the international community, which can put pressure on leaders through trade agreements, the media, and other avenues.

Colonial-era laws still exist in many African nations, even though the imperial powers updated those laws long ago. For example, Nigeria's laws regarding theft are much like England's were in the nineteenth century, yet Great Britain's legal structures have evolved since then. Nigeria's laws can be amended to fit the nation's contemporary social structure and needs.

Along with updating legislation, African nations can ensure that the laws are enforced. Improving the livelihoods (through adequate and prompt payment of wages) and providing proper training for security agents (police, military, and so forth) will make the security sector less susceptible to bribes and corruption.

Finally, implementing government policies that reduce extreme gaps between the wealthy and the poor could help to create a more egalitarian and fair society. This step will be difficult to achieve until corruption, both at the government level and in the security sector, is addressed.

Shifting Boundaries

Physical map boundaries are almost sure to change. The current physical boundaries of nations came largely from an 1885 meeting called the Berlin Conference, where Europeans created them. But the present boundaries fail to take into account the realities and locales of various ethnic and religious identities. People who were forcibly relocated to fit within the colonial powers' ideas of boundaries may wish to return to their former places. The number of displaced persons could potentially be reduced if people could live according to their traditional lifestyles and regions instead of according to what was forced upon them by outsiders.

Women's Empowerment

Over time, women will gain additional opportunities to participate in government, peacemaking, civil society, businesses, and decision making. This is already evidenced by the fact that the continent has had two female presidents, that Tanzania has at present a female vice president, and that economic efforts are shifting to include the full participation of women. Movements to reduce the instances and impacts of

In Ethiopia, a semi-pastoralist people called the Borana have adapted their lifestyle to cope with climate change.

gender-based violence will aid women in gaining full access to their human rights.

Africa's Human Rights in a Global Context

The international community has a vital role to play in Africa's future. This role will be quite different than the colonialist and imperialist ones of the past. Instead, nations outside of Africa will have the opportunity to partner with both governments and grassroots organizations to creatively solve problems. This will mean doing more listening than in the past. It will mean providing resources while allowing Africans the right of self-determination as they solve their own problems in ways they see fit.

Imagine what could happen in the next decades if many nations from around the world collaborate together to promote and support human rights–based initiatives in Africa.

Regional Map of Africa

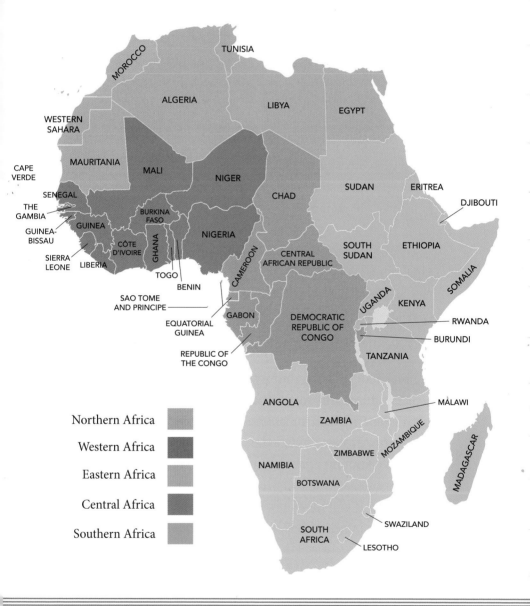

MOROCCO
TUNISIA
ALGERIA
LIBYA
EGYPT
WESTERN SAHARA
CAPE VERDE
MAURITANIA
MALI
NIGER
SUDAN
ERITREA
DJIBOUTI
SENEGAL
THE GAMBIA
BURKINA FASO
CHAD
GUINEA-BISSAU
GUINEA
NIGERIA
SOUTH SUDAN
ETHIOPIA
SIERRA LEONE
LIBERIA
CÔTE D'IVOIRE
GHANA
CENTRAL AFRICAN REPUBLIC
SOMALIA
TOGO
CAMEROON
BENIN
UGANDA
KENYA
SAO TOME AND PRINCIPE
GABON
DEMOCRATIC REPUBLIC OF CONGO
RWANDA
EQUATORIAL GUINEA
BURUNDI
REPUBLIC OF THE CONGO
TANZANIA
ANGOLA
MALAWI
ZAMBIA
MOZAMBIQUE
ZIMBABWE
MADAGASCAR
NAMIBIA
BOTSWANA
SWAZILAND
SOUTH AFRICA
LESOTHO

Northern Africa
Western Africa
Eastern Africa
Central Africa
Southern Africa

 Chronology

1948 The UN creates the Declaration of Universal Human Rights

1961 The First Congress of African Jurists, held in Lagos, Nigeria, asks African governments for an African convention on civil rights with a court and a commission

1965 The International Convention on the Elimination of All Forms of Racial Discrimination is adopted

1966 The International Covenant on Economic, Social and Cultural Rights is ratified; the International Covenant on Civil and Political Rights is also ratified this year

1979 The Convention on the Elimination of All Forms of Discrimination against Women is adopted

1981 The African Charter on Human and Peoples' Rights (also referred to as the Gambul Charter) is adopted in Nairobi, Kenya, by the Organization of Africa Unity (now called the African Union)

1981 The United Nations establishes the Fund for Victims of Torture to help survivors recover and pursue legal action

1984 The Convention against Torture and Other Cruel, Inhuman or Degrading Treatment or Punishment is ratified

1986 The first African Human Rights Day is observed on October 21; the African Union Human Rights Commission convenes

1987 The African Commission on Human and Peoples' Rights is established to "promote, protect, and interpret the rights enshrined under the Charter"

1989 The Convention on the Rights of the Child is adopted

1990 African Charter on the Rights and Welfare of the Child is ratified

1998 The Protocol on African Human Rights Court is adopted

1999 The African Charter on the Rights and Welfare of the Child comes into force

2000 The Constitutive Act of the African Union is signed by the leaders of fifty-three African countries in Lome, Togo

2003 Protocol to the African Charter on the Rights of Women in Africa (Women's Protocol) is adopted

2004 AU signs the Solemn Declaration on Gender Equality in Africa in Addis Ababa, Ethiopia

2004 Court's Protocol enters into force

2005 Women's Protocol enters into force

2006 Convention on the Rights of Persons with Disabilities is held

2006 International Convention for the Protection of All Persons from Enforced Disappearance meets

2009 The African Court delivers its first judgment, ushering in a new level of justice for Africans

2011 Tunisia's Jasmine Revolution starts; revolutions start in Egypt, Libya, and elsewhere in the Middle East, commonly called Arab Spring; a major drought affects the Horn of Africa (Kenya, Ethiopia, Sudan, South Sudan, Somalia, Eritrea, and Djibouti)

2011 The African Children's Charter Committee calls Kenya to account for its failure to register and provide nationality to children of Nubian descent

2012 The eighteenth session of the African Union Summit is held in Malabo, Equatorial Guinea; its theme is "Youth empowerment for sustainable development"

2015 The AU calls this the "Year of Women's Empowerment and Development Towards Africa's Agenda 2063"; the UN passes a Resolution on the Right to Water Obligations (to protect water from pollution and guarantee water rights to displaced people and especially to women); it advocates a human rights–based approach to water rights rather than a commercial approach

2016 The AU deems 2016 the African Year of Human Rights

2016 The African Court convicts former Chadian dictator Hissene Habré of human rights violations; this is the first time a ruler of one African country (Chad) is tried by another country (Senegal); former vice president of DR Congo is found guilty of war crimes against Central African Republic

 Glossary

African Court (The African Court on Human and Peoples' Rights) A court established by African countries to protect the rights of individuals and groups in Africa, continent-wide. It enforces laws created by the African Commission on Human and Peoples' Rights.

animism Traditional African religious and spiritual beliefs (in contrast to Christianity or Islam, and predating these religions).

Arab A person descended from those that come from the Middle Eastern region.

Berbers People who trace their origins from the regions of northern Africa prior to the Arab conquest.

colonialism The practice of one sovereign nation controlling the people and resources of another region for the benefit of the nation in power; colonized regions are called colonies or protectorates.

decolonization The process by which a former colony gains independence and self-determination.

development The process of creating more options for people to pursue different livelihoods; development includes the removal of barriers to choice.

East African Court of Justice (EACJ) An international court established by the eastern African nations of Burundi, Kenya, Rwanda, Tanzania, and Uganda.

extrajudicial killing Putting someone to death outside of formal legal structures.

female genital mutilation/circumcision (FGM/C) Removal of all or part of the female genitalia for nonmedical reasons; human rights groups consider this a form of gender-based violence.

gender-based violence Acts of violence committed based on gender; may include physical, sexual, or psychological harm; typically refers to violence against women, but may also include transgendered people, or less commonly, men.

genocide Actions committed with the purpose of destroying a specific national, ethnic, racial, or religious group; may include killing, forced birth control or sterilization, or forcibly removing children to another group.

human rights Inalienable rights that belong to all human beings, regardless of "nationality, place of residence, sex, national or ethnic origin, color, religion, language, or any other status." All people are entitled to certain rights without discrimination.

imperialism Extending one country's power and influence to others beyond its borders by using diplomacy or military force.

impunity Disregard for justice; when those who commit crimes are not held to account.

Islamist A frequently misunderstood word with multiple meanings including 1) followers of the religion of Islam (Muslims), or 2) extremists who wish to establish a political state based on the religion of Islam, often through violent means.

neocolonialism A condition where a former colony, now independent, continues to be economically and politically influenced by outside powers to a substantial degree. Some call this the final and most dangerous stage of colonialism.

nongovernmental organization (NGO) Organization that functions as a part of civil society and that is not run by a government but provides support to citizens and groups.

referendum A vote on a particular issue.

reparations An attempt to compensate, often in monetary form, for past harms.

resilience The ability to withstand or recover from adversity.

self-censorship When the risks of being punished for free speech are so great that journalists or other media limit their own freedom of speech.

sustainable development Economic development that does not deplete natural resources.

torture To intentionally cause pain or suffering, either physical or psychological, in order to get information, confession, or compliance from the victim; banned by the Geneva Convention, which considers it a war crime.

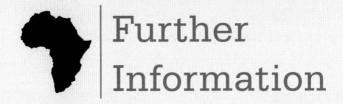

Further Information

Books

Griswold, Eliza. *Tenth Parallel: Dispatches from the Fault Line Between Christianity and Islam*. New York, NY: Farrar, Straus and Giroux, 2010.

Kristoff, Nicholas, and Sheryl WuDunn. *Half the Sky: Turning Oppression into Opportunity for Women Worldwide*. New York, NY: Vintage, 2010.

Mandela, Nelson. *Long Walk to Freedom*. New York, NY: Little, Brown and Company. 2013.

Websites

Child Rights International Network

https://www.crin.org/en/guides/un-international-system/regional-mechanisms/african-committee-experts-rights-and-welfare

This website from Child Rights International Network provides easy-to-find links to virtually all the international organizations that relate to human rights. Click on "Guides" and "UN & International System" to find clear explanations to the "UN rights mechanisms, including what they do, how they operate and how they can be used to advocate for human rights."

CIA World Factbook

https://www.cia.gov/library/publications/resources/the-world-factbook

The Central Intelligence Agency provides extensive facts about each country in the world, including statistics, maps, and information about governance.

US State Department Human Rights

http://www.humanrights.gov

The United States government keeps track of human rights issues worldwide and reports annually on each country.

Bibliography

African Commission on Human and Peoples' Rights. *A Guide to the African Human Rights System*. Pretoria, South Africa: Pretoria University Law Press, 2011. http://www.achpr.org/about/african-hr-system-guide.

———. "Algeria's 5th and 6th Periodic Reports." December 2014. http://www.achpr.org/files/sessions/57th/state-reports/5-2010-2014/algeria_state_report_eng.pdf.

———. "Amnesty International: Human Rights Situation in Africa." October 24, 2011. http://www.achpr.org/sessions/50th/ngo-statements/9/.

African Court of Human and Peoples' Rights. "African (Banjul) Charter on Human and Peoples' Rights." Retrieved June 27, 2016. http://en.african-court.org/images/Basic%20Documents/charteang.pdf.

African Union. "African Aspirations for 2063: The Africa We Want." Retrieved June 27, 2016. http://au.int/en/agenda2063/aspirations.

Al Jazeera News. "Nigeria's Buhari Meets Freed Chibok Girl Amina." May 19, 2016. http://www.aljazeera.com/news/2016/05/nigeria-buhari-meets-freed-chibok-girl-amina-160519173531393.html.

BBC News. "Angola's de Morais Charged over Diamond Book." March 24, 2015. http://www.bbc.com/news/world-africa-32035628.

Central Intelligence Agency (CIA). *The World Factbook*. June 26, 2016. https://www.cia.gov/library/publications/resources/the-world-factbook/index.html.

Child Rights International Network (CRIN). *The UN and the International Human Rights System*. Retrieved June 27, 2016. https://www.crin.org/en/guides/un-international-system/regional-mechanisms/african-committee-experts-rights-and-welfare.

Collins. *Map of the World*. London, UK: Harper Collins, 2014.

Economic Community of West African States (ECOWAS). "Basic Information." 2015. http://www.ecowas.int/about-ecowas/basic-information.

Elmangoush, Najla. "Customary Practice and Restorative Justice in Libya." United States Institute of Peace, May 28, 2015. https://www.usip.org/publications/2015/05/28/customary-practice-and-restorative-justice-in-libya-hybrid-approach.

Human Rights Watch. "World Report 2016: Events of 2015." 2016. https://www.hrw.org/sites/default/files/world_report_download/ wr2016_web.pdf.

Interviews with anonymous international students and NGO workers from Botswana, Côte d'Ivoire, DR Congo, Egypt, Ethiopia, Kenya, Libya, Nigeria, Sudan, Tanzania, and Zimbabwe. May–June 2016.

Ismael, Edna Adan. "Female Genital Mutilation Survey in Somaliland." Retrieved June 26, 2016. http://www.ednahospital.org.

ISSAfrica. *Protocol on the Statute of the African Court of Justice and Human Rights*. July 1, 2008. https://www.issafrica.org/anicj/uploads/Protocol_on_the_Statute_ of_the_ ACJHPR.pdf.

Kaaba, O'Brien. "The Challenges of Adjudicating Presidential Election Disputes in Domestic Courts in Africa." *African Human Rights Law Journal* 15, no. 2 (2015): 329–354. Pretoria, South Africa: Pretoria University Law Press. http://www.ahrlj.up.ac.za/kaaba-o.

Killander, Magnus. "Human Rights Developments in the African Union During 2014." *African Human Rights Law Journal* 15, no. 2 (2015): 537–558. http://www.ahrlj.up.ac.za.

Kitharidis, Sophocles. "Rape as a Weapon of War. *African Human Rights Law Journal* 15, no. 2 (2015): 449–472. http://www.ahrlj.up.ac.za/kitharidis-s.

Lattimer, Mark. "Peoples Under Threat 2016." Minority Rights Group International, 2016. http://peoplesunderthreat.org/wp-content/uploads/2013/10/Peoples-under-Threat-2016-briefing1.pdf.

Mubangizi, John C. "Human Rights Education in South Africa: Whose Responsibility Is It Anyway?" *African Human Rights Law Journal* 15, no. 2 (2015): 496–514. http://www.ahrlj.up.ac.za/mubangizi-jc1.

OHCHR. "Human Rights and the Millennium Development Goals in Practice: A Review of Country Strategies and Reporting." 2010. http://www.ohchr.org/Documents/Publications/HRAndMDGsInPractice.pdf.

———. "Universal Human Rights Index." Retrieved June 26, 2016. http://www.ohchr.org/EN/HRBodies/Pages/UniversalHumanRightsIndexDatabase.aspx.

Ookafor, Obiora Chinedu, and Basil Ugochukwu. "Raising Legal Giants: The Agency of the Poor in the Human Rights Jurisprudence of the Nigerian Appellate Courts, 1990–2011." *African Human Rights Law Journal* 15, no. 2 (2015): 397–420. http://www.ahrlj.up.ac.za.

Pillay, Navanethem. *Working with the United Nations Human Rights Program: A Handbook for Civil Society.* New York and Geneva: OHCHR, 2008. http://www.ohchr.org/EN/AboutUs/CivilSociety/Documents/Handbook_en.pdf.

Sensenig, Peter. *Peace Clan: Mennonites in Somalia.* Eugene, OR: Pickwick Publications, 2016.

South African Human Rights Commission. "TRC Final Report." Retrieved June 26, 2016. http://www.justice.gov.za/trc/report/execsum.htm.

Teicher, Jordan G. "This Is the World's Oldest Human Population." *Slate*, November 4, 2013. http://www.slate.com/blogs/behold/2013/11/04/nicola_lo_calzo_photographs_the_ san_people_of_south_africa_in_his_series.html.

Transparency International. "2015 Corruption Perceptions Index." 2016. http://www.transparency.org/cpi2015.

Tunamsifu, Shirambere Philippe. "The Right to Justice: A Challenge for Survivors of Conflict-Related Sexual Violence in the Eastern Democratic Republic of the Congo." *African Human Rights Law Journal* 15, no. 2

(2015): 473–495. http://www.ahrlj.up.ac.za/tunamsifu-s-p.

UNECA. "Illicit Financial Flows. Report of the High Level Panel on Illicit Financial Flows from Africa." Retrieved June 26, 2016. http://www.uneca.org/content/illicit-financial-flows-africa-track-it-stop-it-get-it.

UNHCR. "Figures at a Glance." June 20, 2016. http://www.unhcr.org/en-us/figures-at-a-glance.html.

UN.org. "Genocide Prevention." March 2015.http://www.un.org/en/preventgenocide/rwanda/about/bgpreventgenocide.shtml.

———. "Universal Declaration of Human Rights." Retrieved June 26, 2016. www.un.org/en/universal-declaration-human-rights/.

US Department of State. Bureau of Democracy, Human Rights and Labor. "Country Reports on Human Rights Practices." 2015. http://www.state.gov/j/drl/rls/hrrpt/humanrightsreport/index.htm#wrapper.

———. "2009 Human Rights Report: Western Sahara." Retrieved June 26, 2016. http://www.state.gov/g/drl/rls/hrrpt/2009/nea/136076.htm.

World Health Organization. "2015 Report." Retrieved June 26, 2016. http://www.who.int.

Index

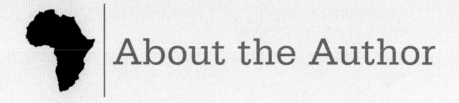# About the Author

Anna Maria Johnson holds an MFA in creative writing from Vermont College of Fine Arts and a BA in studio art from Houghton College. She works in the Writing Center for Graduate and Professional Studies at Eastern Mennonite University, where she has had the privilege of assisting international graduate students with writing research papers in English (for some, English is their second, third, or fourth language!). She also teaches undergraduate writing courses at Eastern Mennonite University and James Madison University in Harrisonburg, Virginia. Several of her students come from some of the countries described in this book.

Johnson is married to a conservation photographer and has two children. The family lives near the North Fork of the Shenandoah River in Virginia.